Teacher Evaluation: Six Prescriptions for Success

Edited by Sarah J. Stanley and W. James Popham

Association for Supervision and Curriculum Development

Printed in the United States of America.

Typeset by Scott Photographics, Inc.

Printed by Edwards Brothers, Inc.

Ronald S. Brandt, *ASCD Executive Editor*
Nancy Modrak, *Manager of Publications*
René M. Townsley, *Associate Editor*

ASCD Stock No. 611-88048

$11.95

Library of Congress Cataloging-in-Publication Data

Teacher evaluation.

   1. Teachers—United States—Rating of. I. Stanley, Sarah J. II. Popham,
W. James.
LB2838.T4 1988   371.1′44   88-19308
ISBN 0-87120-153-4

Teacher Evaluation: Six Prescriptions for Success

Foreword

This is the third year of her probationary period. I have been working with a "new" teacher for the past three years, and now I must decide whether she moves to permanent status or is dismissed. Over the three years I have built trust. We designed her professional growth plan. She has observed my teaching. She has observed other teachers. I have coached her countless times. We have had innumerable preconferences, observations, and postconferences. She has gone to numerous workshops. We have isolated specific skills to work on. She has taken education courses. We have both worked incredibly hard. Yet it hasn't been enough. She is an unbelievably nice person, but she just doesn't have the right stuff.

The hurt I am feeling comes from the realization that this considerable effort has been in vain. Saying that it is important to her to hear the truth, that I owed her that much, doesn't help. I hate being here. Do the consequences of dismissal outweigh the consequences of retention? Do I have the right to interpret and redirect a person's professional career?

I have some lingering doubts about my abilities and efforts in the process. Did I do enough? Did I know enough to effect real change in others? Have I been truly honest throughout the process? Could I have done something differently? Could other strategies have produced the desired effects? I am in pain.

—A principal

One of the contributors to this periodic agony we call summative evaluation (or performance review or appraisal) is the lack of agreement on its purposes and processes. A chapter-by-chapter comparison of each author's views in this volume illuminates the problem. Readers will find that the evaluation process remains ambiguous as evidenced by the authors' diverse perspectives on a variety of issues.

Should we merely evaluate performance, or critique and improve it as well? Can one person do both, or should the two responsibilities of evaluation and supervision be separated? Should evaluation be used to determine merit pay and tenure, or to signal a need for further staff development and training? Should evaluation focus on teaching competencies or on student achievement? How should student achievement be defined and measured?

Who are evaluations supposed to help—the teacher, the student, the administrator, the district personnel office, or the courts? Who should be involved in the evaluation process—students, parents, counselors, other teachers? Should the teacher being evaluated be invited to self-evaluate, or should evaluation be performed only by an administrator who is an "expert"? Who judges the evaluator's ability to evaluate, anyway?

By what criteria and definitions should the performance of professional duties be judged as excellent, adequate, or incompetent? Is it teachers' process-product, research-based behavior? Is it their decision-making and intellectual capacities, or their classroom instruction and managerial skills? Is it their creativity, risk-taking, and experimental abilities, or their demonstration of a set of district- or state-mandated competencies?

How and when should the process take place? Should evaluation be ongoing, biannual, or by March 15? Should it be accompanied by other data gathered from coaching sessions, "walk-throughs," and performance of non-instructional duties? Should it include elements of style, personal qualities, appearance, and communication skills? Should evaluation processes be the same for all teachers, or should they be individualized, based on the teacher's level of development, experience, maturation, and assignment?

And how should the data be collected and reported—with checklists, narratives, matrices, or script tapes? And how should we handle bias? Should we work to enhance and perfect evaluation, or strive to eliminate it?

The authors of *Teacher Evaluation: Six Prescriptions for Success* offer little agreement on these issues. Yet all of them agree on some factors: Evaluation is a rigorous process, and evaluators must be skilled and trained in executing it. All affected parties must be involved in the process. The criteria for judgment must be defined, communicated, and understood by everyone. Supervision must be ongoing. Staff development is a necessary component. There is no substitute for strong instructional leadership and, when handled poorly, evaluation causes suffering for all involved—the teacher, the students, the administrator, the school board, and the superintendent.

S everal school supervisors were recently asked to comment on the problems they encountered in supervising teachers (Sergiovanni 1985). They spoke of supervision as a "pro-forma task," an obstacle to improvement, artificial, detached, impersonal, and too hierarchical. They complained that teachers don't think rationally enough, don't plan, are not responsive to criticism, and are unable to see reality. But when proposing solutions to these problems, the supervisors relied on familiar prescriptions for practice. They emphasized doing better that which they had been doing, trying harder to apply familiar supervisory rationale and techniques, and asserting more intensely the same basic assumptions, characteristics, and designs they currently employ.

The evaluation processes we've produced in the past and which are presented in this book may be the result of the concept of education we have established: hierarchical, isolated, regulated, uniform, and dependent. Perhaps what Elm Hills needs is *not* a revision of the evaluation system to make it more *defensible*, but a revision of the school itself to make it more *viable*. Interestingly, Glickman and Pajak (1986) found that elaborate evaluation systems and efforts were conspicuously absent as descriptors of the numerous effective schools they studied.

I recently met an executive for an environmental engineering firm who told me that in 16 years with his company he had never let an employee go. "In fact," he said, "only one person has left, due to pregnancy." I inquired about his employee evaluation procedure. "We don't evaluate our employees," he responded. "You don't evaluate your people?" I asked with amazement. "Well," he explained, "you must remember that we work in teams, and all employee problems are taken right back to the team for resolution."

Imagine a school organization based on the cultural norms of collegiality, diversity, creativity, and intellectual challenge. Where time is devoted to peer interaction, planning, teaming, and observing each other; where repertoire is enhanced; where intellectual growth is paramount; where teacher participation in making the decisions that affect them—curriculum, instruction, materials, staff development, assessment—is valued; where accountability measures and collecting evidence of their effectiveness is the responsibility of the staff itself. Perhaps we need an optimistic reconceptualization of the processes of teacher evaluation to match the restructured school.

I believe it was Fritz Perls who said, "Abnormal behavior is normal behavior under abnormal conditions." Could the infamous Mrs. Halverson of Elm Hills have been responding to the school conditions under which she worked? If we changed the conditions, would we change the behavior? If we changed the school, would we change the evaluation process?

ARTHUR L. COSTA
ASCD President
1988-89

References

Glickman, C., and E. Pajak. "A Study of School Systems in Georgia Which Have Improved Criterion-Referenced Test Scores in Reading and Mathematics from 1982-1985." Athens, Ga.: Department of Curriculum and Supervision, University of Georgia, June 1986.

Sergiovanni, T. "Landscapes, Mindscapes, and Reflective Practice in Supervision." *Journal of Curriculum and Supervision* 1, 1 (September 1985): 5-17.

Preface

In recent years, we have heard a rising chorus of demands from policymakers at all levels calling for the evaluation of America's teachers. These demands have typically been translated into legislatively enacted statewide teacher-evaluation requirements or board-authorized procedures at the district or state level.

The call for renewed emphasis on teacher evaluation, however, should not be viewed as a request for "more of the same." Increasing numbers of educational policymakers recognize that teacher evaluation, as it has been practiced in the United States, is apt to be perfunctory instead of perceptive. All too often, teacher evaluation is ritualistic rather than rigorous. It fails to yield benefits consonant with its cost. Thus, when today's proponents of tough-minded teacher evaluation demand an expansion of teacher evaluation, they are often calling for innovative, bold evaluative schemes, not merely warmed-over appraisal approaches from the past.

Those public school educators who are responsible for the appraisal of teachers, therefore, are faced with a new and critical challenge, namely, how to design and install a teacher evaluation system that brings about positive benefits to the children we strive to educate. This book is intended to help educators respond to this challenge.

It seems likely that, faced with the current pressures to install defensible teacher evaluation systems, many educators may opt too readily for the first "innovative" teacher appraisal system that they encounter. But, obviously, what is new and different may not be what is good. Those charged with creating new teacher evaluation systems, or renovating old ones, must become more circumspect. Before selecting any one approach (or blending parts from several), they must survey with care a range of alternative teacher appraisal approaches. With few exceptions, circumspection contributes to sound decision making.

In the following pages are six alternative teacher evaluation approaches, each recommended by different individuals. To assist the reader in choosing from among these six approaches, we asked the authors to respond to an identical, imaginary situation involving the appraisal of a teacher. We believe that the fictitious events depicted in this hypothetical vignette are typical of those encountered with regularity throughout the nation's schools. All of the chapter authors were directed to respond to the stage-setting stimulus described in the introduction.

As soon as each chapter was written, it was immediately relayed to a public school practitioner—typically a school principal or central office administrator involved in teacher appraisal—who was asked to supply a "from-the-field" reaction.

We sincerely hope that the six "prescriptions for success" offered in this volume will help educators select or design more defensible teacher appraisal schemes. We believe that readers, abetted by the sometimes compatible, sometimes conflicting views in the following pages, will be able to carve out more sensible teacher assessment schemes. Even in states where statewide teacher appraisal schemes have already been installed, there is often room for district-level augmentation.

We are indebted to the chapter authors for their thought-provoking views and their approximate adherence to deadlines. The authors we asked to contribute to this volume are super busy folks. Nonetheless, not one declined our invitation. They are, clearly, professionals who care about their profession. Our thanks, too, to the practitioners who supplied us with timely and terse reactions to the chapters.

SARAH J. STANLEY
W. JAMES POPHAM
Los Angeles
April 1988

Introduction:
A Dismal Day in
Court

Except for Harriett Halverson and her attorney, December 14 in Municipal Court was a day of disillusionment. Mrs. Halverson had been dismissed as a teacher in the Elm Hills School District five months earlier on grounds of instructional incompetence. Although Mrs. Halverson, a ten-year employee of the district, had been granted tenure seven years earlier, district officials believed that there was sufficient evidence of her incompetence to warrant dismissal.

After a two-day court trial, however, Municipal Judge George Smathers ruled in Mrs. Halverson's favor, chiefly on the grounds that "the district's teacher evaluation program was a simplistic, invalid, and unfair collection of spur-of-the-moment evidence-gathering coupled with arbitrary decision making." Judge Smathers concluded that "although Mrs. Halverson may be insufficiently skilled to be in the classroom, administrators of Elm Hills School District have failed to marshall a meaningful case regarding her instructional competence." The judge ordered her reinstatement as a district teacher and directed the district to compensate her for the days of work she had missed since the beginning of the school year in September.

Sitting in the courtroom to hear Judge Smathers' ruling were four members of the district's five-member school board, including its president, Maria Johnson. Also present were a dozen parents, several of whom had formally complained about Mrs. Halverson's teaching. All of the parents had children who were Mrs. Halverson's pupils during the previous two years. Finally, key district administrators were present, including the superintendent, Dr. Harry Jergens. All of these individuals, most of whom had been present for the entire two-day trial, were simultaneously shocked and disappointed by Judge Smathers' ruling. Without exception, they believed that Mrs. Halverson was an incompetent teacher whose poor teaching truly harmed children.

The object of their outrage, however, soon shifted from Judge Smathers' ruling to the district's apparently flawed teacher evaluation system. After a full hour's heated interchange on the courthouse steps, Board President Johnson delivered a stinging ultimatum to Superintendent Jergens. "Harry," she fumed, "this shouldn't have occurred. Get in some outside consultants who know their stuff and who can design a *defensible* teacher evaluation system from the ground up. Within two months the board will expect a detailed proposal describing a new district teacher evaluation system. Make the plan practical, make it cost effective, and make it consistent with what is known about teacher evaluation. Remember, our district's teacher evaluation system should be designed not only to remove incompetent teachers, but also to improve the effectiveness of all district teachers!"

Stung by this rebuke, Superintendent Jergens wasted little time. After a week's worth of telephone conversations with other superintendents, he had the names of six teacher evaluation authorities from around the country who were supposedly able to provide practical advice to school people as to how to implement a teacher evaluation system. To each of these he issued a letter of invitation to serve as a district consultant. The superintendent's letter (1) described the background events leading to his request and (2) requested a 30- to 40-page description of a practical approach to teacher evaluation that, in each expert's view, would prove serviceable for a "typical K-12 American school district." Superintendent Jergens informed the five experts that he would either adopt one of their approaches in its entirety or selectively choose elements from more than one approach.

The next six chapters contain the responses to Superintendent Jergens' invitation.*

---

*All individuals named in this vignette are fictitious. The scenario was devised specifically to serve as a stimulus to the teacher evaluation experts whose views are presented in this volume.

1 Evaluation for Enhancing Instruction: Linking Teacher Evaluation and Staff Development

THOMAS L. MCGREAL

One of the few enduring initiatives in education is the often strident call for "new and improved" teacher evaluation systems. Whether the call for change is spurred by the angry reaction to some local problem, as in Elm Hills, or is provided by a legislated school-reform movement, the pressure to build better ways to evaluate classroom teachers is pervasive and consistent. Unfortunately, the pressure emerging from both of these settings is often driven by an urgency that does not allow or encourage the careful planning necessary for any change activity to succeed. While the outcome to the Harriet Halverson case was clearly unsatisfactory, it can be the impetus for generating the commitment and resources needed to address a number of issues linked to the teacher evaluation process. The first and most important task is to channel this energy from the negative focus of a "defensible" system to a more positive force that can be applied to the development of a plan in which teacher evaluation is but one ingredient.

Teacher Evaluation as Part of a Bigger Plan

One of the biggest problems Elm Hills faces is that the urgency for improved evaluation procedures is being driven by motives that can be det-

Thomas L. McGreal is Associate Professor, College of Education, University of Illinois, Urbana-Champaign.

rimental to the development of a productive and useful system. A recurring theme in almost all successful evaluation systems is the importance of establishing a clear understanding of the purposes of the system, which must then be reflected in procedures and processes (McGreal 1983, Murphy 1987, Wise and Darling-Hammond 1984). The Elm Hills administrators and board are calling for an evaluation system that will meet a relatively specific purpose— improving their ability to appropriately document and judge incompetent teaching so the district will never again be unable to dismiss a "bad" teacher. While this is a justifiable and acceptable function of an evaluation system, it is but one of a number of important purposes. In fact, the literature on successful evaluation gives it little support as an important or acceptable purpose (Harris 1986, Iwanicki 1981, McGreal 1983, Medley et al. 1984).

Although perspectives differ, most writers (Bolton 1973, Denham 1987, Harris 1986, Redfern 1980) seem to agree that the major purposes of an evaluation are to:

1. Provide a process that allows and encourages supervisors and teachers to work together to improve and enhance classroom instructional practices.

2. Provide a process for bringing structured assistance to marginal teachers.

3. Provide a basis for making more rational decisions about the retention, transfer, or dismissal of staff members.

4. Provide a basis for making more informed judgments about differing performance levels for use in compensation programs such as merit pay plans or career ladder programs.

5. Provide information for determining the extent of implementation of knowledge and skills gained during staff development activities and for use in judging the degree of maintenance of the acquired knowledge and skills.

Each of these purposes alone serves a clear function. But when we look at them as a set of purposes for a single evaluation system, they can be overwhelming. Each purpose demands a set of practices and requirements that adds complexity and "weight" to the system. That actual or perceived weight can dramatically lessen the full and active participation of both administrators and teachers. Their willingness to be involved and to choose to fully participate is absolutely crucial to the success of an evaluation plan (McGreal 1983, Sergiovanni and Carver 1980, Wagoner and O'Hanlon 1968).

It is imperative that Elm Hills first establish exactly the purposes of its evaluation system. Most school districts back off from addressing purpose #4 in that they do not have, or are unlikely ever to have, compensation programs that are driven by performance evaluation data. Most states that have statewide compensation programs have developed an evaluation scheme that must accompany the plan and thus takes away the necessity for the local district to have its evaluation system meet this purpose. (See McGreal 1987 for further discussion of building evaluation systems for use within compensation programs.)

While there is growing attention to addressing the needs of marginal teachers (Sweeny and Manatt 1984), the majority of schools with successful teacher evaluation programs have decided that remedial issues can be addressed within their regular procedures rather than using a set of rules and guidelines built specifically for marginal staff members. Certainly, there are programs for marginal teachers in a number of schools that are viewed as successful (Manatt 1987). But there is a growing feeling that a set of special procedures for marginal teachers sets a tone that is not generally conducive to positive administrator-teacher relationships. This is an example of the "weight" of a system. The more evaluation materials are loaded with procedures and language that are heavy with remedial or punitive overtones, the less likely people are to have positive attitudes about evaluation (Harris 1986, Zelenak 1973, Zelenak and Snider 1974). Because the impetus for change in Elm Hills has come from a perceived lack of attention in dealing correctly with a marginal teacher, it is especially important that the district step back and look rationally at the possible costs of putting a heavy emphasis on procedures and practices for working with the least able teachers. Why build an evaluation system for the few Harriett Halversons when there is considerable evidence that the emphasis on remediation and dismissal proceedings can have a debilitating influence on the development of helping, growth-oriented relationships with the 99 percent of faculty members who are not Harriett Halverson (Harris 1986, McGreal 1983, Medley et al. 1984)?

As in most school districts, Elm Hills' "problem" with Harriett Halverson was not necessarily the fault of the evaluation system. It can be attributed more to the knowledge, skills, and attitudes of the evaluators than to the system itself. Not that the system isn't important; actually, it's far more important than people often think (McGreal 1983). It is the system's procedures and practices that allow or encourage what happens between teachers and administrators. The bottom line of effective evaluation is the quality of what happens when the administrator and teacher get together. Whenever possible, the system should not get in their way. Elm Hills officials should be encouraged to take a minimalist's view toward building their evaluation system. In many respects it should be built backwards. Start with the bottom of the system, the teacher and administrator sitting down and talking together, and build from there. More and more local districts are realizing that if they design a system around effective supervisory and teaching behaviors, and if appropriate training is provided to the administrators and teachers, then a single evaluation system can adequately serve purposes 1, 2, 3, and 5.

Meeting multiple purposes through a single system seems best accomplished when there is a clear commitment to identifying a major, overriding purpose—in this case, the improvement and enhancement of classroom instructional practices. In a sense, this is our bigger plan. Evaluation systems work best when they are viewed as a subset of a bigger movement—a districtwide commitment to the enhancement of classroom instruction. Establish the major goal first, and then build an evaluation system that grows logically from that goal.

In many ways we have tried to make evaluation too complicated. From the minimalist's perspective, all we are trying to do is put in place a process that allows and encourages two adults to get together and talk about teaching. Recent staff development research seems to clearly support the notion that the more people talk about teaching, the better they get at it (Griffin and Barnes 1986, Sparks 1986). Unfortunately, the average school setting does not encourage much "teaching talk" to occur. The only two places where it can happen to any great extent are through staff development activities and through the conversation that is generated by teacher evaluation. These two sources of teaching talk are legitimate and adequate for improving instruction. The job of a school district is to provide staff development opportunities that foster teaching talk and to employ an evaluation system that is both complementary and supplementary to staff development. This is the way in which evaluation and development are most logically linked. As stated in purpose 5, the evaluation system of a district becomes the mechanism for monitoring staff development training and the vehicle for maintaining the instructional momentum generated by training functions.

Both the literature and experiential evidence suggest that evaluation systems focusing primarily on instructional enhancement are almost always accompanied by the necessary levels of accountability (McGreal 1983, Medley et al. 1984, Wood and Lease 1987). On the other hand, systems built from an attitude of "defensibility," heavy with accountability mechanisms, generally lack support or encouragement for growth in instructional practices (Harris 1986, Medley et al. 1984, Murphy 1987). This attempt to focus on instructional enhancement does not mean that the charge given by the Elm Hills board has been forgotten. Rather, this should be viewed as an attempt to expand the opportunities that are available when redesigning an evaluation system.

Necessary Ingredients for Launching Instructional Enhancement Efforts

Leadership Density

The role of strong leadership in the development of effective evaluation systems is well documented (Iwanicki 1981, McGreal 1983, Wise and Darling-

Hammond 1984). It appears that this necessary leadership is manifested in several ways. The most obvious need appears to be leadership that emanates from the top. While much of the effective schools literature points to the importance of the principal in providing instructional leadership at the school level, there is increasing evidence that the role of the superintendent and central office staff members is every bit as crucial to instructional improvement efforts (Murphy and Hallinger in press). Outside consultants have long held that the likelihood for successful implementation of a school improvement effort is in direct proportion to the amount of involvement and commitment shown by the superintendent. Successful leadership from the top must be active leadership. Superintendents and central office staff members must be physically and emotionally involved in the schoolwide process of planning, developing, and implementing a local instructional improvement plan, especially the staff development and staff evaluation components.

While it is necessary to have strong leadership from the top, it is not sufficient. Leadership must be dispersed deliberately throughout the organization; it does not appear to be a natural phenomenon. At the local level, this is one of the main purposes served by having strong staff involvement in the committee or advisory group process. The members of these groups develop and display their leadership by influencing the rest of the staff. This depth becomes increasingly important the more dramatic or threatening the proposed program may be.

Depth of leadership seems to be best obtained by establishing a relatively small (7 to 10 members) instructional advisory group. Group members are selected on the basis of their influence and credibility with their peers; they need not be representative of the entire school district, but they should be active association or union members. Their influential standing appears to be more important than where they are located within the district. It is also advisable to have one board member in this group. This gives the board member the chance to become as knowledgeable as staff members about the group's recommendations, and it gives the group an advocate when recommendations are brought to the board.

For maximum leadership and continuity, this group should be active for at least three to five years. Group members then become the "experts" in instruction and can serve as instigators of or reactors to instructional initiatives. The makeup, the focus, and the continuity of the group help to ensure the depth of leadership so important to successful instructional enhancement efforts.

Knowledge of the Literature

If a district is going to give itself the best chance to put together effective evaluation and staff development practices, it is crucial that at least one person or one group be responsible for knowing what the literature, research, and discussions of best practices are saying about effective programs and practices. The knowledge about effective teaching and supervision, successful teacher evaluation, and staff development has grown dramatically in recent years. It is virtually impossible for the average professional to keep up with the rapid changes in current practices. It demands a systematic, focused, and coordinated effort with the full commitment of the district behind it. The purpose of this effort is to be sure that the district knows the available options and is assured that it is working on the cutting edge of effective programs. It helps the district feel that it is in the best possible position to match its needs with what is available. While most schools end up adapting what they learn to better fit their unique setting, at least they are doing it from an informed opinion.

A Districtwide Sense of Priorities and an Appropriate Time Frame

Although we know little about the Elm Hills school district, we can assume quite a bit. As in most other school districts, recent school improvement efforts at local, state, and federal levels have created significant problems for Elm Hills. These problems are not the result of Elm Hills doing too little to "improve"; rather, it is likely that Elm Hills is doing, or having to do, too much.

The events of the most recent school-reform movement have spawned a series of local, state, and federal initiatives that, while well-meaning for the most part, have in fact spread the resources and energies of districts and staffs to the point that most of these new efforts have become counterproductive. There is only so much we can ask of the people who work in our schools. Right now, we are creating a generation of teachers and administrators who are unable to give the time and energy to ever see a program or a new initiative through to maturity. No sooner do schools implement a new emphasis than the next effort is started. Suddenly, energy and resources must be diverted to the new project. Consequently, teachers and administrators are never able to get any closure on projects because they can never stay with them long enough.

Districts like Elm Hills need to take the time to determine what is most important to them and then to be sure that top priorities receive their major commitment. A first step for Elm Hills would be to develop some sense of what exists in the district right now. This can often be accomplished by establishing a "war room." In effect, this room contains a map of every major initiative, program, special project, and program emphasis in the district— everything going on that takes time, money, or energy from the district and its staff. With this coordination, it often becomes easier to see where resources are going and the relationship between where they are going and what is viewed as being most important.

This chapter assumes that there is no higher priority in a district than resources provided for the enhancement and improvement of classroom instructional practices. Of all the things a district can do, resources placed in instructional efforts often produce the highest dividends in terms of student learning (Good et al. 1975). It is imperative that districts establish this emphasis on instruction as a high priority.

A new program requires at least a three- to five-year commitment from a district to have a chance to succeed. The necessary ingredient here is the district's willingness and ability to stay with an effort and not make any other major commitments that could detract from it. An appropriate time frame for instructional enhancement programs is essential. Schools must be willing to be judged on the basis of the quality of fewer programs rather than feel that their quality must and can be determined by the quantity of programs and initiatives they are trying to support. If Elm Hills is unwilling or unable to make the kind of commitment necessary to see these initiatives through to maturity, then its efforts will quickly dissipate.

Structured Staff Development

Centrality can benefit instructional staff development activities (Murphy and Hallinger in press). To assure successful and lasting instructional enhancement efforts through teacher evaluation and staff development, core training should be provided to all teachers and administrators in a district.

Part of the responsibilities of the instructional advisory group would be to build a "framework for teaching" drawn primarily from three sources: (1) reviews of the research on teaching that are based on the empirical studies linking teacher behaviors to student cognitive achievement, i.e., the teacher effects research; (2) teacher behaviors that are generated by applying theory-based concepts to teaching situations, i.e., Hunter "models"; (3) the use of "conventional wisdom," i.e., those things that experienced teachers feel are important and have generated from consensus building among district staff members. What emerges is a picture of what the school district thinks effective teaching looks like. How the framework is built and which sources are used ensure that the dimensions of teaching listed probably do make a difference in promoting student learning. (See Medley et al. 1984 for a more detailed discussion of building a reasonable and supportable set of teacher performance dimensions for use in instructional improvement activities.) At this point, the framework can become the driving force behind the instructional enhancement efforts of the district.

The first use of the framework is as a guide for evaluating various staff development options. In many respects, the 1980s has been the era of staff development. The number of people involved in staff development and the number of programs, workshops, institutes, seminars, conferences, and courses have increased dramatically. Consequently, the problem facing local school districts is not the availability of staff development but trying to decide what makes most sense for the district right now. Unfortunately, most districts have adopted the view that if a little staff development is good, a lot would be even better. The result is a smorgasbord of staff development activities supposedly designed to meet the needs of individual teachers and administrators. What happens, however, is that energies and resources are spread over so many programs that only small groups participate in any one activity. No single program has enough support to keep it alive. The people who attend a particular program end up being able to talk only with each other because they are the only ones with the understanding and terminology to make sense out of what was presented.

The presence of the framework and a commitment to a focused, structured staff development approach can help improve this situation. The framework becomes the guide for evaluating instructional staff development options. The advisory group recommends which programs seem to best reflect what the district has determined are the most important dimensions of teaching. These dimensions then become the core offerings in which all staff members participate. As an example, assume members of the advisory group, either through past exposure or through judgments based on their literature review, feel very comfortable about teaching behaviors or strategies drawn from the work of Madeline Hunter (1984). The framework then built would likely show a heavy reliance on terminology and practices associated with Hunter or her advocates. Consequently, the advisory group would recommend that a staff development program featuring the Hunter work be required of all teachers and administrators.

This is a clear move away from the volunteer notion of staff development. Certainly there are teachers and administrators who will profit less or perhaps not at all from required staff development; however, most training activities are not going to make people worse. Required participation helps build consistency between and among the different organizational levels and buildings in a district. Too often, instructional enhancement efforts have been eroded because only certain buildings or teachers (more elementary than secondary) choose to volunteer. It should be made clear that this common exposure to staff development is not designed to force or require all teachers to act and think alike; rather, teachers should share common language and dispositions (Raths and Katz 1985) for use in facilitating and encouraging more frequent teaching talk. Thus, districts need to select trainers who have a good understanding of all the complexities of teaching and are not dogmatic about a particular approach.

There are other approaches besides Hunter's to shape the framework or to make decisions about staff development opportunities. Equally influential is the work associated with the teacher effects research. (See Wittrock 1986 for the best and most recent review of the research on teaching.) When this more empirical approach is used by districts, such staff development programs as TESA and Classroom Management Training (Emmer et al. 1980) can be the core programs.

As faculty members complete the core training, other staff development programs can be offered. But the primary responsibility of staff development should be to first give everyone in the district an introduction to the knowledge, skills, and understandings that have driven the development of the district's framework for teaching. Mandated participation may seem like a top-down situation that contradicts popular beliefs about successful change strategies, but the most effective strategies may be a combination of the top-down and bottom-up movements (Clark et al. 1984, Glickman 1987). In this type of instructional improvement focus, it is perfectly legitimate for a district advisory group to make decisions about instructional directions. The key for successful implementation is heavy staff involvement in reviewing and commenting on the framework and significant involvement in making decisions about the best ways to begin to implement the recommended staff development programs and the new teacher evaluation system.

Figure 1.1 is a framework for teaching developed by the Gwinnett County (Georgia) schools. As is recommended here, the framework was built first, then an appropriate staff development program was designed. The framework will then be used as the performance criteria within the newly built teacher evaluation system. In this way the framework becomes the most logical link between staff development and teacher evaluation.

Successful efforts to enhance instruction through staff development and teacher evaluation can be developed without any or all of those recommended ingredients being present. However, experience indicates that the likelihood of successful maintenance of important instructional initiatives is significantly increased if districts take the time to develop these ingredients before rushing into any major redesign of teacher evaluation programs.

Components of an Evaluation System that Complements Instructional Enhancement

The next logical step is to construct an evaluation. Elm Hills needs to ensure that the time spent developing and putting in place the necessary ingredients for instructional enhancement is not wasted. The evaluation system must complement what the district wants it to be and do (McGreal 1983). Too often, developers who spend time espousing a strong growth-oriented

Figure 1.1
A Framework for Teaching

Planning

A. Develops and prioritizes long- and short-term objectives within curriculum guidelines
  1. Identifies specific prerequisite skills and/or knowledge necessary to accomplish the objective.
  2. Plans instruction as needed to promote student mastery of prerequisite skills and knowledge.
  3. Prepares written lesson plans to support instructional objectives.
  4. Incorporates cognitive levels of learning: knowledge, comprehension, application, analysis, synthesis, and evaluation.
  5. Plans appropriate evaluation.
B. Evaluates, selects, and modifies resources and activities
  1. Reviews resources.
  2. Selects resources and activities and activities that match objective(s).
  3. Selects resources and activities that match the learner(s).
  4. Selects resources and activities that provide a variety of learning modalities.

Implementing

A. Provides initial focus for the lesson
  1. Clearly communicates specific learning objectives to students.
  2. Provides a context for objectives by one or more of the following:
     a. presenting an overview or outline of how information fits together
     b. reviewing related previous work
     c. describing the purpose, rationale, or relevance for what is to be learned
  3. Captures student attention through active involvement.
B. Delivers lesson
  1. Uses appropriate delivery strategy(ies)—ways of providing information for students to acquire the learning—for example: lecture, discussion, inquiry, or cooperative group learning.
     a. presents definitions, examples, illustrations, and concrete points of reference
     b. uses aids and materials that effectively support the presentation
     c. emphasizes critical or important areas of the topic by explicitly stating or highlighting their importance
     d. models learning processes
     e. provides relevant examples and models of higher-level thinking by verbalizing the process of analysis, synthesis, and evaluation
     f. summarizes or reviews during the lesson to provide continuity
  2. Relates new ideas to previous or future learning.
     a. provides simple examples first and then moves to more difficult or complex examples
     b. relates learning to relevant life experiences
     c. points out similarities and differences in learning
     d. uses associations and analogies
  3. Organizes content for presentation of the lesson.
     a. presents information in a logical sequence, such as: moving from simple to complex, and moving from concrete to abstract
     b. organizes the presentation of content into blocks or steps based on the ability of the students and the complexity of the material
  4. Uses questions to promote understanding.
     a. creates the expectation of being called on by eliciting responses from volunteers and nonvolunteers
     b. asks clearly stated questions that are relevant to the objective(s)

  c. provides cues to prompt, correct, or expand student answers
  d. asks students to explain answers and clarify answers
  e. pauses after asking a question to provide wait-time for student responses
  f. asks questions before calling upon specific students, thereby encouraging all students to formulate answers
  g. asks questions that require knowledge, comprehension, application, analysis, synthesis, and evaluation

C. Provides guided practice.
 1. Conducts relevant teacher-directed group practice activities after presenting new information or skills
 2. Provides guided practice on new learning in amounts that are appropriate to the complexity of the content, to logical division of the content, and to the ability of the student (for example: small bits of information for complex content or for low-ability students).
 3. Moves among the students to give assistance during guided practice.
 4. Continues guided practice until most students are capable of mastering the objectives.

D. Provides independent practice.
 1. Assigns independent practice after successful guided practice.
 2. Assigns appropriate independent practice through in-class or homework activities.
 3. Differentiates independent practice assignments based on learner needs.

E. Monitors instruction.
 1. Generates relevant observable behavior—written, verbal, and physical—by involving students in practice activities and by asking group and individual questions.
  a. varies the types of responses generated, such as asking students to: respond on scratch paper, take notes, tell another student, respond chorally, or use signal responses
  b. stimulates covert involvement of students by using strategies such as: directing all students to think of an example, asking them to remember an experience, or asking them to mentally prepare to describe a picture or model
 2. Interprets student responses to determine opportunities for praise, prompts, extensions, and corrective feedback.
  a. observes students' facial expressions and other nonverbal behaviors to determine if further clues or explanations are needed
  b. observes students for initial engagement after making assignments
  c. listens to verbal responses to check understanding, progress, and involvement
  d. moves among students to check progress, understanding, and involvement and to give assistance during individual or group work
 3. Provides feedback on student responses.
  a. provides specific feedback on responses that are correct and on why they are correct
  b. provides feedback to students by repeating, paraphrasing, applying, or extending their correct responses
  c. provides specific feedback on responses that are incorrect and on why they are incorrect
  d. takes corrective action, such as: giving hints, using different words and examples, reteaching, creating smaller steps, and employing alternative instructional materials when students make incorrect responses
  e. provides individual students with opportunities to give correct answers by dignifying incorrect responses, by providing prompts, and by returning later to the student for a chance to repeat the correct response

F. Closes lesson by using an appropriate strategy(ies).
 1. Restates the objective that has been stressed in the lesson.   *Continued*

Figure 1.1 (continued)

2. Asks a student to summarize the lesson or state the objective.
3. Summarizes the main points of the lesson.
4. Asks questions to determine whether students are thinking about what they have learned and putting ideas together in their minds.
5. Associates material the students have learned that day to previous material studied or to future learning.
6. Provides an interesting "clincher" to bring the lesson to an effective close and leave the students with something to think about.
7. Relates what the students have studied that day to the overall unit itself.
8. Tells the students what they will be studying the next day and perhaps how it relates to what they have been studying during this day's lesson.

Evaluating

A. Provides formative evaluation that measures student progress toward objective(s).
1. Observes students' facial expressions and other nonverbal behaviors to determine if further clues or explanations are needed.
2. Listens to verbal responses to check understanding, progress, and involvement.
3. Generates relevant observable behavior—written, verbal, and physical—by involving students in practice activities and by asking group and individual questions.
4. Moves among students to check progress, understanding, and involvement.
5. Provides criteria that allow students to measure their own progress toward an objective.

B. Provides summative evaluation that measures student achievement of objective(s).
1. Provides evaluation that matches learning objectives.
2. Provides evaluation that is appropriate for the learner(s).
3. Maintains evaluation records for each student.
4. Communicates evaluation results to student.
5. Uses evaluation results to plan for subsequent instruction.

Classroom Climate

A. Organizes learning environment to maximize student time on task.
1. Organizes and arranges classroom to facilitate learning.
2. Makes smooth transitions from one activity to another.
3. Maintains an orderly system for housekeeping duties—attendance, passes, announcements, distributing and collecting materials and homework assignments.

B. Maintains behavior that is conducive to learning
1. Clearly defines and communicates behavior expectations to students.
2. Monitors behavior and provides appropriate feedback to students.
3. Deals effectively with inappropriate behavior.

C. Helps learners develop positive self-concepts.
1. Focuses on student behavior rather than personality.
2. Communicates a high degree of appropriate academic praise for all students.
3. Treats sensitive situations with discretion.
4. Encourages participation from all students.
5. Accepts diverse opinions.
6. Establishes mutual respect between teacher and students.
7. Conveys warmth, friendliness, and enthusiasm.

Source: This framework for teaching is used with the permission of the Gwinnett County Schools, Lawrenceville, Georgia. The framework's opening philosophy statement and an explanation of how it is and is not to be used are not included here.

position finally construct one that fails to reflect that stance. The only way the district can be assured that the system allows and encourages good supervision and evaluation is if the advisory committee continuously compares the new system against what is known about improving and enhancing instruction through evaluation (Duke and Stiggins 1986).

Successful evaluation and supervision depends on the quality of what happens between the teacher and evaluator (McGreal 1983). Many of the variables necessary to make this one-on-one relationship productive revolve around the type of training given participants and the attitudes they hold and display during their involvement in evaluation (Darling-Hammond 1983). Thus the quantity and quality of the supervisor's skills gained through training and experience and the degree that the supervisor and teacher trust each other are the main determiners of the effectiveness of evaluation. Nevertheless, for the supervisor's skills to be used effectively, the system must allow and promote their application. Additionally, credibility and trust are gained primarily through the behavior and action displayed during evaluation activities. The system itself makes a difference and thus deserves considerable thought and attention.

A number of reviews focus on what evaluation can and should be (McLaughlin 1984, Reyes 1986, Stiggins 1986, Stiggins and Bridgeford 1985) and on what components should make up successful teacher evaluation systems (Conley 1987, Duke and Stiggins 1986, McGreal 1983, 1987, Wise et al. 1984). It appears that an evaluation system is more likely to support teacher and teaching growth if it:

1. Includes clear criteria, established with significant teacher involvement, that reflects the district's framework for looking at and talking about teaching.

2. Provides opportunity for increased teacher involvement within the actual functioning of the system.

3. Provides opportunity to use multiple sources of data to ensure the fullest possible picture of teaching.

4. Allows and encourages feedback activities that have been shown to encourage professional growth.

Establishing Clear Criteria

An essential element of any effective evaluation system is a clear, visible, and appropriate set of evaluation criteria. As Strike and Bull (1981) indicate, it is the responsibility of a school district and the right of a teacher to have an explicit set of criteria or expectations that define the teacher's role. In addition to meeting legal responsibilities, local criteria also serve as a template to compare performance. This increases consistency among the different evaluators and provides general guidelines for teachers and supervisors to use in directing their enhancement efforts. It is likely that part of the problem Elm Hills faced was an unclear and poorly defined set of criteria that prevented them from pointing to previously developed teaching behaviors that were part of their expectations for teachers.

In the best of situations, evaluation criteria are driven by the framework for teaching. Using this concept, the criteria should be built by a consensus approach (Medley et al. 1984) that is directed by the instructional advisory committee (or a similar group, such as a subcommittee of the evaluation committee). This criteria building or framework development generally includes choosing the dimensions of teacher performance that are thought to be crucial and then defining each dimension provisionally by specifying behaviors whose occurrence in the classroom are examples of their use (Medley et al. 1984). The framework in Figure 1.1 is a good example of a generally accepted set of performance dimensions and accompanying behaviors. Certainly, this is only one example of what a district like Elm Hills might construct, but it offers an excellent outline for comparison.

The criteria in Figure 1.1 are drawn primarily from the teacher effects research and Hunter's work. Often the researchers and the developers of the most popular staff development models urge that their work should be kept separate from evaluation activities. Their arguments are legitimate in that the effects research and other views of effective teaching are not designed for evaluation and have been misused. Yet it seems unrealistic to suggest that in the real world of schooling this clear division can be maintained. If a staff development program designed to improve or enhance classroom instruction is made available to teachers and supervisors, then in effect it is legitimized as containing behaviors important to student learning. If ways of teaching have been viewed important enough to allocate energy and resources to train staff members, then they are significant enough to be included in the district's criteria. Actually it all depends on the way the criteria are used. If they are viewed for what they should be—a framework for directing actions and not a set of rules that must be displayed—then it is logical and necessary that the components of effective teaching form the basis for our criteria.

The framework presented in Figure 1.1 focuses on only the classroom instructional practices of teachers. While this may be the most important part of teachers' jobs, it does not cover all of their responsibilities. A full presentation of evaluation criteria should include administrative, personal, and professional criteria as well as actual classroom performance criteria. All may not be equally important in the overall evaluation of a teacher, but they do contribute to the complete view of what a teacher is minimally expected to do and to be. Figure 1.2 is an example of a set of minimum expectations established by a local school district. These minimums are stated in a series of relatively general statements. In districts that have chosen this format, these

Figure 1.2
A Statement of Minimum Expectations

An integral part of both tenured and nontenured staff members' employment in the school district is an ongoing appraisal by their supervisor of their ability to meet minimum expectations. As appropriate to the various jobs performed by staff members in the school district, the minimum expectations include, but are not necessarily limited to, the following:

1. Meets and instructs the students in the location at the time designated.
2. Develops and maintains a classroom environment conducive to effective learning within the limits of the resources provided by the district.
3. Prepares for classes assigned, and shows written evidence of preparation upon request of the immediate supervisor.
4. Encourages students to set and maintain high standards of classroom behavior.
5. Provides an effective program of instruction in accordance with the adopted curriculum and consistent with the physical limitations of the location provided and the needs and capabilities of the individuals or student groups involved.
6. Strives to implement by instruction the district's philosophy of education and to meet instructional goals and objectives.
7. Takes all necessary and reasonable precautions to protect students, equipment, materials, and facilities.
8. Maintains records as required by law, district policy, and administrative regulations.
9. Makes provisions for being available to students and parents for education related purposes outside the instructional day when necessary and under reasonable terms.
10. Assists in upholding and enforcing school rules and administrative regulations.
11. Attends and participates in faculty and department meetings.
12. Cooperates with other members of the staff in planning instructional goals, objectives, and methods.
13. Assists in the selection of books, equipment, and other instructional materials.
14. Works to establish and maintain open lines of communication with students, parents, and colleagues concerning both the academic and behavioral progress of all students.
15. Establishes and maintains cooperative professional relations with others.
16. Performs related duties as assigned by the administration in accordance with district policies and practices

The appraisal of these minimum expectations will typically be made through a supervisor's daily contact and interaction with the staff member. When problems occur in these areas, the staff member will be contacted by the supervisor to remind the staff member of minimum expectations in the problem area and to provide whatever assistance might be helpful. If the problem continues or reoccurs, the supervisor, in his or her discretion, may prepare and issue to the staff member a written notice setting forth the specific deficiency with a copy to the teacher's file. In the unlikely event that serious, intentional, or flagrant violations of these minimum expectations occur, the supervisor, at his or her discretion, may put aside the recommended procedure and make a direct recommendation for more formal and immediate action.

general statements are literally kept separate from the more specific performance criteria as exemplified in Figure 1.1. These behaviors are evaluated as needed; they are not automatically a part of the supervisor-teacher discussions during classroom teaching. This is the essence of the concept of separating administrative and supervisory behavior during evaluation (McGreal 1982, 1983).

Establishing clear criteria is crucial to building successful teacher evaluation systems. These criteria help satisfy a number of important ingredients.

1. Clear criteria offer the district and the teacher legal and due process safeguards (Peterson 1983, Strike and Bull 1981). In effect, this assures that accountability demands can be met while focusing on instructional enhancement.

2. Performance criteria follow recommended procedures to provide the necessary guidelines for assuring consistency and focus for evaluation and enhancement efforts (Acheson and Gall 1987, Duke and Stiggins 1986, Darling-Hammond et al., 1983, McGreal 1983).

3. When developed from the district's framework for teaching, the criteria allow the evaluation system to be the instrument for implementing and maintaining the framework-driven staff development initiatives (Wood and Lease 1987).

Involvement Within the System

Current research consistently suggests that the strong involvement of teachers is necessary if evaluation systems are to be successful (Duke and Stiggins 1986, Huddle 1985, Stiggins and Bridgeford 1985). Because the press for an improved, defensible evaluation system in Elm Hills came from the top, it is especially important that this component be incorporated into their plans. On the surface, the concept of teacher involvement seems straightforward. Most districts include teachers in planning efforts and then assume that this meets the need for participation. Such early, limited involvement is useful, but it does not address the issue seriously enough. Teachers must feel a sense of involvement within the internal workings of the evaluation system (Huddle 1985, Ruck 1986, Wise and Darling-Hammond 1985).

The two most obvious ways to increase teachers' participation in the evaluation system are to:

1. Have teachers become actively involved in data collection and feedback via collegial supervision, peer coaching, and teacher mentoring.

2. Build mechanisms within the system that allow for more teacher participation as they work with administrators.

The most logical and practical method is to construct processes that encourage more administrator-teacher cooperation. This is not to discourage the development of supervisory relationships, for there is clearly an expanding literature on the usefulness and potential of such activities (Alfonso and Goldberry 1982, Cruikshank and Applegate 1981, Garawski 1980, Glatthorn 1984, Joyce and Showers 1981, Little 1985). However, for the average school, the use of these approaches still seems a long way off. For all of the increasing discussion about more collegial involvement, there are still not enough exemplars or empirical evidence to suggest whether it has an impact on teaching and learning (Sparks 1986). Additionally, there are many unanswered questions about how local districts can handle the costs, logistical problems, and attitude adjustment necessary to make these processes function effectively. This is not to deny the potential, but in looking realistically at the movement, local districts should assume that the great majority of supervision and evaluation of instruction is going to result from interaction between a teacher and an administrator rather than between teachers.

This leaves school districts to find ways within the evaluation system to increase teacher-administrator collaboration. Evaluation practices should involve individual goal-setting activities that occur between teachers and administrators and should form the major focus for what they do together (Acheson and Gall 1987, Iwanicki 1981, McGreal 1983, Redfern 1980). Goal setting has been a recommended practice in teacher evaluation since the management-by-objectives (MBO) movement hit education (Lewis 1973). Since then it has gone through several adaptive formats (Iwanicki 1981, Redfern 1980). The most widely accepted format currently in use is generally labeled the Practical Goal Setting Approach (McGreal 1983).

A set of beliefs about supervisors, teachers, and teaching is basic to goal setting. The primary reason for developing or redesigning an evaluation system is to enhance classroom instruction. As such, the major reason for setting goals is to allow the supervisor and the teacher the chance to establish a narrow, more workable focus for their efforts. Viewing teachers and administrators realistically, it is unlikely that either group is going to be able to commit significant amounts of additional time to the evaluation process. In moving to new evaluation procedures that require considerably more time and energy, supervisors and teachers are seldom told what activities and responsibilities may be dropped to provide the additional time. Rather, the additional time is always viewed as an add-on to what they are already doing. Many potentially effective systems have failed because they placed unrealistic demands on the time and resources of the people involved. Consequently, goal setting attempts to focus on improving the quality, rather than the amount, of time spent between supervisor and teacher.

Basically, the most effective goal setting starts with a conference between the administrator and the teacher at the beginning of the school year. (Some districts prefer doing this toward the end of the preceding year.) The purpose of the conference is to establish the goal or goals that will be the major focus for what the teacher and the administrator do together. All other evaluation activities between the two parties are now driven by these goals and plans for attaining them. The general rule is that the more talented and experienced the teacher, the more the administrator relies on the teacher in establishing goals. The less talented and less mature the teacher, the more directive the administrator needs to be. This process encourages the implementation of a number of contemporary supervisory practices such as developmental supervision (Glickman 1981) and differentiated supervision (Glatthorn 1984). The key is that the goal setting is a cooperative process that occurs between two people and forms the basis for a working relationship that carries through the entire evaluation period. Too often schools establish professional growth and improvement plans that require teachers to produce goals at the beginning of the year or following the receipt of their final summative evaluation, share them with their supervisor, and then get together at the end of the year for the teacher to tell the administrator what has been done. That is a paper exercise that gives the illusion of involvement. To be effective, goal setting must be based on a continuing collaboration between two people. This is the essence of supervisory behavior.

In the best of situations, the established goals are clearly the focus of attention. The goals are driven whenever possible by the previously developed framework for teaching or by the established performance criteria. This does not mean that only the goals are given attention. Certainly, the framework/criteria are always there symbolically. But it is impossible to see and judge all that is represented in a full description of effective teaching. The administrator must use professional judgment to decide what is most important and how best to encourage a focus on those things. Supervision and evaluation are long-term processes. The average teacher is a competent professional who does not need to be continuously monitored on such a wide range of behaviors that there is never time for focusing on one or two variables that can have lasting impact.

Once the goals are established, they become the goals of both the teacher and the administrator. Plans are built from the notion of what "we" can do to help meet the goals. Feelings of joint responsibility and cooperation are not natural phenomena. Standard evaluation practices have cast teachers and administrators into an adversarial rather than a cooperative role. But through training for both teachers and administrators and a system that allows it to happen, cooperation can be achieved successfully. Functioning and effective goal-setting systems exist in hundreds of school districts like Elm Hills.

The actual recommended practices for effective goal setting—such as how many goals should be set, how the plans are built, what the goals should look like, and how to handle situations where the teacher and administrator disagree about what goals should be set—are detailed elsewhere (McGreal 1983). Suffice it to say that the development of individual goals and the cooperative development of a plan for addressing them can satisfy a number of important components of successful evaluation systems. For instance:

1. Goal setting provides a real opportunity for teacher involvement within the system, not just in the planning stages.

2. Goal setting allows administrators and teachers to focus on a narrower, more manageable set of behaviors or skills that recognizes the limits of available time and energy.

3. Goal setting and the development of specific plans to address each goal allows administrators to use the variety of supervisory skills that are available to them through staff development.

4. Individual goal setting allows administrators to satisfy due process requirements by providing a focused remediation plan when teacher competence is marginal.

5. Goal setting allows for the directed, structured remediation activities that are a necessary part of any required documentation when teacher dismissal on the grounds of incompetence is contemplated.

6. The cooperative development of goals allows teachers and administrators far more opportunities to build trust and credibility between them.

7. Goal setting encourages focusing on knowledge, behaviors, and skills that have been generated through staff development programs, thus encouraging the implementation and maintenance of these programs.

8. The plans that are built from the goals allow administrators considerably more flexibility in using different methods and alternative sources of data. This gives them far more opportunity to exercise their professional judgment about what is best for that particular teacher.

The Use of Alternative Sources of Data

To make the best possible judgments about the quality of job performance, the fullest picture of that performance must be developed. While observation has been the dominant method of collecting formal data about teaching, there are other data-gathering methods that can be helpful, if not essential, in establishing an effective evaluation effort. Teaching and learning are complex acts that occur in many forms and contexts. To be studied as fully as possible, teaching needs to be looked at in a variety of ways. The credibility of administrators is enhanced by their being able to understand, demonstrate, and recommend different alternatives for pursuing goals.

There are at least eight recognized techniques for collecting data for evaluating instructional practices: paper-and-pencil test, self-evaluation, parent evaluation, peer evaluation, student performance, student evaluation, artifact collection, and observation. Actually, none of the eight alone has been proven to be reliable for making summative judgments. However, data from multiple sources increases reliability (Epstein 1985). While all eight of these methods have some potential use, problems such as practicality and questionable reliability make it essential that local districts decide which make the most sense for them given their particular needs and environment. The most seriously questioned methods include paper-and-pencil tests (Medley et al. 1984, Quirk et al. 1973), self-evaluation (Brighton 1965, McGreal 1983), parent evaluation (Becker and Epstein 1982, McGreal 1983), peer evaluation (Bergman 1980, Cohen and McKeachie 1980, McGee and Eaker 1977), and student performance (Millman 1981, Medley et al. 1984, Stiggins 1988).

Three data-gathering methods seem to receive most of the attention. In the judgment of many, students are a powerful source of data about classrooms (Farley 1981, McNeil and Popham 1973, Walberg 1969). However, the average teacher is uncomfortable with the concept (McGreal 1983). They generally lack faith in students' ability to accurately rate a teacher's performance. It appears that the kind of data collected and how they are used are the key elements in the acceptability and usefulness of student input. Evaluators can obtain reliable student information if they concentrate on describing life in the classroom rather than making judgments of the teacher. Walberg (1974) reinforced this view when he indicated that a series of studies have demonstrated that student perceptions of the classroom learning environment can be measured reliably. The key phrase is "student perceptions of the learning environment," not student perceptions or judgments of the teacher's performance.

A number of available instruments focus on perceptions of life in the classroom (Anderson 1973, Walberg et al. 1973). They offer excellent examples of the difference between asking students to respond to descriptive statements ("I feel free to ask and answer questions in this class") rather than evaluative statements ("The teacher is not very well organized"). This concept can also drive the development of instruments that are used only in a single situation where the teacher and administrator feel that it would be useful to get some student feedback about one of the goals. This type of data is much less threatening to teachers since it does not ask students to evaluate them. Sharing this information also promotes high levels of teaching talk between the teacher and the supervisor. The general recommendation for using student feedback is that it would be a required part of nontenured teachers' plans, but it would be used with tenured teachers only as it fit a particular goal.

Artifact collection, or materials sampling, is another data source gaining popularity. Time as a variable of learning has become a more visible concept, and the way teachers and students spend their instructional time in classrooms has been studied in a more systematic and accurate fashion (Rosenshine 1980). Current data suggest that K-12 students spend as much time interacting with teaching artifacts as they do being directly taught by the teacher (McGreal and Collins 1985). These realities of classroom life make it imperative that teacher evaluation procedures include the systematic analysis and discussion of classroom materials (McGreal 1983).

Teaching artifacts include all instructional materials used to facilitate learning. This includes everything from textbooks, workbooks, and supplementary texts to learning kits, maps, audiovisual aids, films, dittoed material, study guides, question sheets, worksheets, problem sets, quizzes, and tests. Typically, teachers assume the responsibility for collecting the artifacts for an entire teaching unit, or for a two- to three-week period from a single class. Following the collection, the teacher and supervisor review, analyze, and discuss the materials.

Much research is needed to learn more about the effect of teacher artifacts on teaching and learning. At this point, the most positive benefit seems to be the high level of technical-professional talk it generates between teachers and supervisors. While frameworks for use in analyzing artifacts are available (McGreal et al. 1984), it should be assumed that the major impact of artifact collection and analysis will be in the area of formative evaluation. Nontenured teachers should be required to go through at least one artifact collection each year. Its use with tenured teachers would be determined by its appropriateness to the goals established between the teacher and the administrator.

The last of the most-recommended sources of data about teaching is classroom observation. The quality of observations and the ways administrators collect and share data with teachers are still the major factors in the success and effectiveness of teacher evaluation systems. Much of the usefulness of observation can be attributed to the fact that it is a learned skill. In reviewing many of the excellent sources available regarding classroom observation (Acheson and Gall 1987, Good and Brophy 1987, Hyman 1986), there appear to be four practical ways for administrators to improve their observation and feedback skills.

1. The reliability and usefulness of classroom observation is directly related to the amount and type of information administrators have before the observation. (This suggests training in the techniques that are embedded in clinical supervision.)

2. The narrower the focus administrators use in observing classrooms, the more likely they will be able to accurately describe the events relating to that focus. (This is an encouragement for goal-setting models and the development of a districtwide framework for teaching that help focus attention on valid teaching behaviors.)

3. The impact of observational data on administrator-teacher relationships is directly related to the way data are recorded during observation. (Observers must learn to record descriptively rather than judgmentally and should be introduced to the different types of observation instruments available.)

4. The impact of observational data on administrator-teacher relation-

ships is directly related to the way feedback is presented to the teacher. (This suggests the need for training in conferencing skills and the ability to write summative evaluations that contain supporting facts for all value terms used.)

Observation has been the dominant method for collecting data about teaching and is a requirement in most goal-setting systems. Because teachers generally accept observations and because it is reasonably reliable (Medley et al. 1984), classroom observation should remain the major source of data used in teacher evaluation. However, districts like Elm Hills must be prepared to provide the necessary training to make it as useful as it can and should be.

Encouragement and training in the use of alternative sources of data is clearly a commonality of most effective evaluation systems. Common sense dictates that the most reliable and valid professional judgments are going to be made by administrators in direct relation to the amount and quality of data available. The three alternatives discussed in some detail are most appropriate within the context of formative evaluation. Taken together, they can provide the fuller, richer picture of performance that is necessary for making summative judgments. Evaluations must ultimately be made on the basis of an administrator's best professional judgments (Popham 1987); the use of a variety of input can help add credibility and reliability to those judgments.

The Nature and Type of Supervisory and Evaluative Feedback

Feedback's importance to the success of an evaluation system is well documented (Acheson and Gall 1987, Duke and Stiggins 1986, Hyman 1986). Unfortunately, the seriousness of this component is often overlooked. The quality and quantity of training available for supervisors has increased dramatically. Without exception, districts like Elm Hills need to be sure to establish a staff development program that is geared directly to the attitudes, knowledge, and skills required to function effectively within their system. Minimally, this means training in the use of the variety of sources of data allowed within the system, the ability to collect accurate data through observation, and, as is suggested in this section, ways of handling written and verbal feedback. Too often, staff development activities are focused on the techniques for data collection only. Yet the actual point of contact between teachers and administrators is not data collection but feedback.

There are two ways in which districts can assure themselves that they are doing everything possible to direct teacher feedback toward the enhancement of instructional practices. The first involves providing training in productive feedback. It is crucial for administrators to have an overall perspective on the value and the purposes of feedback. In effective evaluation systems, teachers must be involved, encouraged, reinforced, and made to feel successful. Teachers only change their behavior when they want to! As Hunter (1980) indicates, "The same principles of learning apply to teachers as apply to students." The ability to provide accurate and helpful feedback is a learned skill. For example, there are a number of relatively simple concepts that can significantly increase the positive effect of feedback on teachers:

• How to open and close conferences (Kindsvatter and Wilen 1981).

• Where and when conferences should be conducted (Goldhammer et al. 1980).

• Physical arrangements most conducive to effective communications (Hyman 1986).

• Use of direct and indirect supervisory styles (Acheson and Gall 1987).

• How to handle negative feedback (Goldhammer et al. 1980).

• Understanding teachers' different stages of development and the impact this has on the type and nature of feedback (Glickman 1981).

• Different types of supervisory conferences and when they are most appropriate (Hunter 1980).

These examples apply primarily to verbal feedback given to teachers. While not as much attention has been given to written forms of feedback, many of the same principles apply.

One of the major dilemmas faced by administrators is that they are generally required to produce written final evaluations that are clearly summative. The difficulty of this activity is compounded by the fact that virtually all of the training they receive is designed around formative techniques. Administrators are continually reminded to collect data descriptively rather than judgmentally and to provide verbal feedback through clinical models that encourage formative techniques such as collaborative supervision, indirect styles, and problem-solving formats. At the conclusion of the evaluation activity, administrators then find themselves in the predicament of having to use formatively collected data to make summative judgments. Certainly the ability to construct useful narratives based on classroom observations is a skill that would undoubtedly carry over to evaluation reports. But there is an important and obvious difference between descriptive narratives and the use of value terms as required in summative evaluation write-ups.

Borrowing from work originally done in dealing with written critiques in art (Meux 1974), all written and verbal summative feedback should operate from a simple model for valuing. Basically, the simple model suggests that no value statement or value term should be used unless it is accompanied by example, anecdote, illustration, or description. These become the facts to support the value. (See McGreal 1983 for a fuller explanation of the model for providing written or verbal feedback.) The concept allows administrators to use the descriptive data collected during the supervision/evaluation process (the carrying-out of the plans in a goal-setting model) as the facts to support the values that must accompany the summative portion of evaluation.

The second way districts can promote the wise use of feedback is to make sure that the procedures and instruments within the system are conducive to productive feedback. The most frequent inhibitors of productive feedback are the timing and type of feedback that occurs at the end of the evaluation activity and the required instrumentation that shapes the feedback.

In Elm Hills as well as other districts, the final activity of the evaluation experience is the written summative document. It becomes for many teachers their last and usually most vivid contact with the process. Recent experience gives the impression that perhaps this write-up should not be the highlight of the evaluation activity. No written evaluation should ever be composed by the evaluator until after the final conference. Most administrators speak better than they write. Administrators should enter final conferences armed with all the data that have been accumulated throughout the evaluation period—including the original goals, all records of contact between the two that grew out of these goals, and any other data that accumulated as the administrator and teacher interacted. During the analyzing, interpreting, and joint interaction in the conference, the administrator can verbally elaborate on points, use examples, provide nonverbal cues, and generally address issues in a fuller, more expressive and understandable manner than time, space, and ability allow when trying to write the same things. At the conclusion of the conference there can be a joint summing up of what has occurred and what may happen next. The administrator can then write up what was discussed and put it in the teacher's box for review and signature. There should be no surprises for the teacher since everything of importance should have been fully discussed in the conference. Too often, write-ups are read by the teacher before the conference. Since written statements can so easily be misunderstood, the teacher is forced into a defensive posture before the conference is even under way. The highlight of the evaluation experience then becomes the conference, not the content of the write-up. This is a classic example of how little things within the system can have a major impact on the success of the evaluation process.

The second and perhaps most powerful deterrent to productive feedback is a final evaluation document with some form of rating scale. No single idea or concept has been more detrimental to successful teacher evaluation than the rating scale. There are a number of documented reasons for eliminating ratings from teacher evaluation.

• Because rating scales can provide the basis for some numerical score and thus offer some comparative data, they have an air of empiricism or objectivity about them. Actually, rating scales, because of their high-inference nature, are the most subjective of measures (Medley et al. 1984).

• From a measurement perspective, there are severe limitations to the usefulness of rating scales in dealing with performance evaluation. This is primarily due to their general lack of reliability over time (Medley et al. 1984), their lack of validity (Soar and Soar 1980), and their high susceptibility to the halo effect (Cooper 1981).

• The use of rating scales as a measure of teacher performance turns the criteria into rules rather than guidelines. This is clearly a violation of what the effects research or the Hunter work was designed to be or do (Brandt 1987).

• The presence of rating scales forces comparisons between and among teachers. This situation is especially damaging to administrator-teacher relationships because, with the rare exception of those districts that have some form of compensation plans based on evaluation, the ratings or comparisons are never used and serve no purpose other than to aggravate people once a year (McGreal 1983).

• The criteria upon which most ratings are made do not and cannot offer clear enough specificity to provide any meaningful or reliable discriminations. This is especially true when administrators are asked to rate teachers using multiple positive categories (i.e., superior, excellent, satisfactory). Since every teacher wants to be superior, administrators are continually put in a position of having to provide definitions between superior and excellent. It is virtually a no-win situation for the rater (Medley et al. 1984).

To provide administrators a chance to use feedback in more positive and constructive ways, evaluation write-ups should be based on narratives and not ratings. The narrative format allows more opportunity for clearer explanations of values and a more focused approach to areas that are most relevant for each individual. The narrative provides a less complex and "lighter" approach to evaluation while still providing the opportunity for descriptive problem identification and remedial recommendations. Certainly, training in descriptive writing and practice in the use of facts to support values is crucial. But again, these are learned skills that can be mastered by administrators. Elm Hills must recognize that all of their "defensibility" concerns can be met while constructing a system that allows administrators a chance to build productive, more collaborative relationships with teachers. The use of narratives for final summative judgments is just one more example of how systems can be built to serve different purposes while still complementing the enhancement of instruction.

In reviewing the needed ingredients and the recommended components discussed in this chapter, Elm Hills must continually go back to the fundamental purposes of evaluation. Elm Hills officials must maintain a view of the bigger picture. The impact of teacher evaluation can go far beyond meeting some legal or political requirements. The ingredients and components addressed here deal with the fundamental issue of enhancing classroom instructional practices. Clearly, it is possible to build processes for increasing the level of talk about teaching through the integration of staff development and teacher evaluation. Programs and systems based on these propositions are functioning effectively in schools right now. It does make a difference, and it can in Elm Hills as well.

References

Acheson, K., and M. Gall. *Techniques in the Clinical Supervision of Teachers*. New York: Longman, 1987.

Alfonso, R., and L. Goldsberry. "Colleagueship in Supervision." In *Supervision of Teaching*, edited by T. Sergiovanni. Alexandria, Va.: Association for Supervision and Curriculum Development, 1982.

Anderson, G. *The Assessment of Learning Inventory*. Halifax, Nova Scotia: Atlantic Institute for Education, 1973.

Becker, H., and J. Epstein. "Parent Involvement: A Study of Teacher Practices." *Elementary School Journal* 83 (1982): 85-102.

Bergman, J. "Peer Evaluation of University Faculty." *College Student Journal* 14 (1980): 55-58.

Bolton, D. *Selection and Evaluation of Teachers*. Berkeley, Calif.: McCutcheon, 1973.

Brandt, R. "On Teacher Evaluation: A Conversation with Tom McGreal." *Educational Leadership* 44 (April 1987): 20-26

Brighton, J. *Increasing Your Accuracy in Teacher Evaluation*. Englewood Cliffs, N.J.: Prentice-Hall, 1965.

Clark, D., L. Lotto, and T. Astuto. "Effective Schools and School Improvement: A Comparative Analysis of Two Lines of Inquiry." *Educational Administration Quarterly* 20 (1984): 41-68.

Cohen, P., and W. McKeachie. "The Role of Colleagues in the Evaluation of College Teaching." *Improving College and University Teaching* 28 (1980): 147.

Conley, D. "Critical Attributes of Effective Evaluation Systems." *Educational Leadership* 44 (April 1987): 60-64.

Cooper, W. "Ubiquitous Halo." *Psychological Bulletin* 90 (1981): 218-244.

Cruikshank, D., and J. Applegate. "Reflective Teaching as a Strategy for Teacher Growth." *Educational Leadership* 38 (April 1981): 553-554.

Darling-Hammond, L., and A. Wise. "Teaching Standards, or Standardized Teaching?" *Educational Leadership* 41 (October 1983): 66-69.

Denham, C. "A Perspective on the Major Purposes and Basic Procedures for Teacher Evaluation." *Journal of Personnel Evaluation in Education* 1 (1987): 29-32.

Duke, D., and R. Stiggins. *Five Keys to Growth Through Teacher Evaluation*. Portland, Oreg.: Northwest Regional Education Laboratory, 1986.

Emmer, E., C. Evertson, and L. Anderson. "Effective Classroom Management at the Beginning of the School Year." *Elementary School Journal* 80 (1980): 219-231.

Epstein, J. "Home and School Connections in Schools of the Future: Implications of Research on Parent Involvement." *Peabody Journal of Education* 62 (1985): 18-41.

Farley, J. "Student Interviews as an Evaluation Tool." *Educational Leadership* 39 (December 1981): 184-187.

Garawski, R. "Collaboration Is Key: Successful Teacher Evaluation Not a Myth." *NASSP Bulletin* 64 (1980): 1-7.

Glatthorn, A. *Differentiated Supervision*. Alexandria, Va.: Association for Supervision and Curriculum Development, 1984.

Glickman, C. *Developmental Supervision*. Alexandria, Va.: Association for Supervision and Curriculum Development, 1981.

Glickman, C. "Good and/or Effective Schools: What Do We Want?" *Phi Delta Kappan* 69 (1987): 622-624.

Goldhammer, R, R. Anderson, and R. Krajewski. *Clinical Supervision*. 2d ed. New York: Holt, Rinehart, and Winston, 1980.

Good, T, C. Biddle, and J. Brophy. *Teachers Make a Difference*. New York: Holt, Rinehart, and Winston, 1975.

Good, T., and J. Brophy. *Looking in Classrooms*. 4th ed. New York: Harper and Row, 1987.

Griffin, G., and S. Barnes. "Using Research Findings to Change School and Classroom Practice: Results of an Experimental Study." *American Educational Research Journal* 23 (1986): 572-586.

Harris, B. *Developmental Teacher Evaluation*. Boston: Allyn and Bacon, 1986.

Huddle, G. "Teacher Evaluation—How Important for Effective Schools?" *NASSP Bulletin* 69 (1985): 58-63.

Hunter, J. "Knowing, Teaching, and Supervising." In *Using What We Know About Teaching*, edited by P. Hosford. Alexandria, Va.: Association for Supervision and Curriculum Development, 1984.

Hunter, M. "Six Types of Supervisory Conferences." *Educational Leadership* 37 (1980): 404-412.

Hyman, R. *School Administrator's Faculty Supervision Handbook*. Englewood Cliffs, N.J.: Prentice-Hall, 1986.

Iwanicki, E. "Contract Plans." In *Handbook of Teacher Evaluation*, edited by J. Millman. Beverly Hills, Calif.: Sage, 1981.

Joyce, B., and B. Showers. "The Coaching of Teaching." *Educational Leadership* 38 (1981): 4-10.

Kindsvatter, R., and W. Wilen. "A Systematic Approach to Improving Conferencing Skills." *Educational Leadership* 38 (April 1981): 525-526.

Lewis, J. *Appraising Teacher Performance*. West Nyack, N.Y.: Parker, 1973.

Little, J. "Teachers as Teacher Advisors: The Delicacy of Collegial Leadership." *Educational Leadership* 43 (November 1985): 34-36.

Manatt, R. "Lessons From a Comprehensive Performance Appraisal Project." *Educational Leadership* 44 (April 1987): 8-14.

McGee, J., and R. Eaker. "Clinical Supervision and Teacher Anxiety: A Collegial Approach to the Problem." *Contemporary Education* 49 (1977): 24-30.

McGreal, T. "Effective Teacher Evaluation Systems." *Educational Leadership* 39 (January 1982): 303-305.

McGreal, T. *Successful Teacher Evaluation*. Alexandria, Va.: Association for Supervision and Curriculum Development, 1983.

McGreal, T., E. Broderick, and J. Jones. "Teacher Artifacts." *Educational Leadership* 42 (1984): 30-33.

McGreal, T., and C. Collins. "Seatwork: A Perspective for Teachers and Supervisors." Champaign: University of Illinois, 1985.

McGreal, T. "Identifying and Evaluating Teachers." In *Establishing Career Ladders in Teaching*, edited by P. Burden. Springfield, Ill.: Charles Thomas Publishers, 1987.

McLaughlin, M. "Teacher Evaluation and School Improvement." *Teachers College Record* 86 (1984): 193-207.

McNeil, J., and J. Popham. "The Assessment of Teacher Competence." In *Second*

Handbook of Research on Teaching, edited by R. Travers. Chicago: Rand-McNally, 1973.

Medley, D, H. Coker, and R. Soar. *Measurement-Based Evaluation of Teacher Performance.* New York: Longman, 1984.

Meux, M. "Teaching the Art of Evaluating." *Journal of Aesthetic Education* 8 (1974): 85-95

Millman, J., ed. *Handbook of Teacher Evaluation.* Beverly Hills, Calif.: Sage, 1981.

Murphy, J. "Teacher Evaluation: A Comprehensive Framework for Supervisors." *Journal of Personnel Evaluation in Education* 1 (1987): 157-180.

Murphy, J., and P. Hallinger. "The Superintendent as Instructional Leader: Findings From Effective School Districts." *Journal of Educational Administration* (in press).

Popham, J. "The Shortcomings of Champagne Teacher Evaluations." *Journal of Personnel Evaluation in Education* 1 (1987): 25-29.

Peterson, D. "Legal and Ethical Issues of Teacher Evaluation: A Research-Based Approach." *Educational Research Quarterly* 7 (1983): 6-16.

Quirk, T., B. Witten, and B. Weinberg. "Review of Studies of the Concurrent and Predictive Validity of the NTE." *Review of Educational Research* 43 (1973): 39-113.

Raths, J., and L. Katz. "Dispositions as Goals for Teacher Education." *Teaching and Teacher Education* 3 (1985): 47-53.

Redfern, G. *Evaluating Teachers and Administrators: A Performance Objectives Approach.* Boulder, Colo.: Westview Press, 1980.

Reyes, D. "Bringing Together Teacher Evaluation, Observation, and Improvement of Instruction." *The Clearinghouse* 59 (1986): 256-258.

Rosenshine, B. "How Time is Spent in Elementary Classrooms." In *Time to Learn,* edited by C. Denham and A. Lieberman. Washington, D.C.: U.S. Government Printing Office, 1980.

Ruck, C. *Creating a School Context for Collegial Supervision: The Principal's Role as Contractor.* Eugene: Oregon School Study Council, 1986.

Sergiovanni, T., and F. Carver. *The New School Executive.* 2d ed. New York: Harper and Row, 1980.

Soar, R., and R. Soar. "Classroom Behavior, Pupil Characteristics, and Pupil Growth for the School Year and the Summer." *JCAS Catalog of Selected Documents in Psychology* 19 (1980): 200-210.

Sparks, G. "The Effectiveness of Alternative Training Activities in Changing Teacher Practices." *American Educational Research Journal* 23 (1986): 217-225.

Stiggins, R. "Teacher Evaluation: Accountability and Growth Systems—Different Purposes." *NASSP Bulletin* 70 (1986): 51-58.

Stiggins, R. Revitalizing Classroom Assessment. *Phi Delta Kappan* 70 (1988): 363-368.

Stiggins, R., and N. Bridgeford. "Performance Assessment for Teacher Development." *Educational Evaluation and Policy Analysis* 7 (1985): 85-97.

Strike, K., and B. Bull. "Fairness and Legal Context of Teacher Evaluation." In *Handbook of Teacher Evaluation,* edited by J. Millman. Beverly Hills, Calif.: Sage, 1981.

Sweeny, J., and R. Manatt. "A Team Approach to Supervising the Marginal Teacher." *Educational Leadership* 41 (April 1984): 25-27.

Wagoner, R., and J. O'Hanlon. "Teacher Attitude Toward Evaluation." *Journal of Teacher Education* 19 (1968): 471-475.

Walberg, H. "Predicting Class Learning: A Multivariate Approach to the Class as a Social System." *American Educational Research Journal* 4 (1969): 529-540.

Walberg, H., E. House, and J. Steel. "Grade Level, Cognition, and Affect: A Cross-Section of Classroom Perceptions." *Journal of Educational Psychology* 74 (1973): 250-260.

Walberg, H., ed. *Evaluating Educational Performance.* Berkeley, Calif.: McCutcheon, 1974.

Wise, A., and L. Darling-Hammond. "Teacher Evaluation and Teacher Professionalism." *Educational Leadership* 42 (1984): 28-33.

Wise, A., L. Darling-Hammond, M. McLaughlin, and H. Bernstein. *Teacher Evaluation: A Study of Effective Practices.* Santa Monica, Calif.: Rand Corporation, 1984.

Wittrock, M., ed. *The Handbook of Research on Teaching.* 3d ed. New York: Macmillan, 1986.

Wood, F., and S. Lease. "An Integrated Approach to Staff Development, Supervision, and Teacher Evaluation." *Journal of Staff Development* 8 (1987): 52-55.

Zelenak, M. "Teacher Perceptions of the Teacher Evaluation Process." Doctoral diss., University of Iowa, 1973.

Zelenak, M, and B. Snider. "Teachers Don't Resent Evaluation—If It's for the Improvement of Instruction." *Phi Delta Kappan* 55 (1974): 348-349.

MARY LOU BARGNESI

From the Practitioner's Point of View...

Practitioners view theories and models from a very different perspective than those who create them. We must live with the practice of conceptual frameworks and with their consequences.

As with so many other issues in education, our problem lies not so much in knowing what to do or how to do it, but in striking a balance between theory and practice. In this instance, the balance must be struck between an evaluation system focused on improving instruction and one that is effective in making difficult employment decisions, although these goals are not mutually exclusive.

McGreal has outlined the elements of a successful model focused on improving instruction. One might argue with some of the specifics and the timeline. In general, though, the model is admirable because it builds involvement and empowerment of teachers, is linked to staff development, and is committed to developing articulate, sensitive administrators schooled in the arts of conferencing and narrative writing.

Yet McGreal has not fully accepted the consequences of a system that by its nature and constraints must serve two purposes: supervisory and evaluative. By avoiding the dreaded "rating scale," his model does not strike that crucial balance between helping teachers grow and biting the bullet when they will not or cannot grow.

The exclusive use of narrative weakens the model when it is applied to the very small percentage of teachers who do not belong with children. We would much rather deal with that group in another way. The problem is that most districts must make the document work for teachers of all categories. As McGreal has stated, a totally different approach for marginal or poor teachers adds undesirable weight to the model. That brings us back to balance and the narrative. No matter how carefully written or factually documented, narrative is open to interpretation. Unless there is a clear, behaviorally anchored rating scale tied to the criteria McGreal suggests, employment decisions must be based on the subjective interpretation of the narrative. A rating scale clarifies expectations and provides a snapshot of where a teacher stands. The evaluator wants to know, the teacher wants to know, and most definitely the union and legal folk want to know: Is this teacher good enough to stay or bad enough to go? A rating scale can help answer that question. The narrative details the reasons behind the ratings.

Mary Lou Bargnesi is currently Principal of Lyme School and Curriculum Coordinator for Regional School District No. 18 in Lyme, Connecticut. She has also taught English at the secondary level and served as a high school administrator.

Evaluation is a hard task for supervisors and for teachers. A combined rating scale and narrative helps keep all of us honest and provides balance. When used correctly, it helps prevent some of the softness that can creep into narratives, and it avoids the tendency for a supervisee to interpret written data in the most favorable light. Experience has taught me that numbers often speak louder than words, especially with those who are experiencing difficulty.

Finally, whether working with a marginal teacher or a superior instructor, the combined narrative/rating scale provides a stronger tool for encouraging interaction between administrators to confront and clarify their assessments, which improves dialogue with teachers. The combined scale provides a basis for teachers to judge their self-evaluation against that of the supervisor. In the hands of sophisticated evaluators, the clarity and depth provided by the instrument help move all of us toward our ultimate goal of improved instruction.

2 Create Rather Than Await Your Fate In Teacher Evaluation

When I read Superintendent Jergens' request for advice, the first thought that came to mind was, "Good, better, best. Never let it rest. Until good becomes better and better becomes best!" This should become the slogan for teacher evaluation, although good-better-best is a relative phenomenon. As in medicine, research is always revealing a new cure or technique that eventually becomes the new "best."

There are many examples of the good-better-best syndrome in education. The most obvious was the expectation that impoverished, culturally disadvantaged, and handicapped students could not learn. Research, however, has demonstrated that these students, if taught properly, can learn and achieve as well as any other students. Moreover, we now accept the assertion that almost all students can learn to think, a skill formerly believed to be the domain of the gifted.

We also now believe that most (not all) people of average or above average intelligence who are willing to expend the required effort can become reasonably effective teachers. In addition to ability and a willingness to try, those wanting to be effective teachers must have:

• Adequate preparation in their content area.

Madeline Hunter is Professor, Department of Education, University of California, Los Angeles.

32

- Knowledge of the psychological generalizations related to cause-effect relationships in teaching and learning.
- Skills (usually developed through coaching) in translating that knowledge into performance behavior in a classroom.
- Demonstrated the use of judgment as to when specific educational techniques and generalizations about learning should or should not be used.

This chapter, unlike others in this book, is written from a clinician's orientation. The focus and examples are derived from research-based clinical experiences: working with and evaluating teachers for many decades to transform conscientious beginners into superb professionals. To avoid professional myopia, this chapter reflects advice and experiences solicited from 400 principals, superintendents, and supervisors who participated in my supervision and evaluation seminars in the summer of 1987. The folks in the Elm Hills School District can be assured that this approach is grounded in the reality of public schools today.

The focus of this book is on teacher evaluation, but the validity of evaluation depends on what happens before the evaluation. To make a high-stakes assessment of a teacher on the basis of one or two observations is a major violation of assessment procedures. Consequently, the major part of this chapter focuses on prior activities (programs of inservice, coaching, and formative evaluation) that contribute to making the final evaluation valid and defensible.

The first section of this chapter identifies basic assumptions in teacher evaluation. Then, procedures for translating those assumptions into reality are described. Evaluation program prerequisites and the skills that must be acquired are discussed. Next, a cohesive staff development-teacher evaluation program is detailed in terms of critical elements of the program and the preparation of evaluators. A timeline for inservice, formative coaching, and supervision that culminates in summative evaluation concludes the chapter.

Several key terms are used in this chapter:

- Staff development: a total program for enhancing professional effectiveness.
- Inservice: instruction designed to supply information and develop skills that can be translated into professional practice.
- Coach: a colleague who observes and gives feedback about an episode of teaching.
- Supervisor: a person with major responsibility for increasing professional skills through inservice, observation, and growth-evoking feedback.
- Evaluator: a person designated to summarize the quality of professional performance over a period of time, and assigned the responsibility for determining a teacher's future status.

Basic Assumptions in Teacher Evaluation

Sophisticated supervisors and evaluators should base teacher evaluation on the following assumptions.

1. Teaching is a learned profession, not a genetic endowment. (Granted, some learn more easily than others.)

2. Many principles governing effective teaching can be described, taught, observed, and documented in practice.

3. Artistry beyond the science of teaching exists, can be observed, but seems not to be predictably acquired through direct instruction.

4. All teachers (and all administrators) should continue to grow in professional effectiveness and artistry as a condition of employment.

5. Increasing the quality of educational practice should be encouraged, stimulated, and demanded by formative and summative evaluation.

6. Career opportunities and psychological incentives for continuing growth must be available to excellent teachers. Stimulation and incentives for growth should be provided for "average" teachers. Compassionate but rigorous and effective remediation should be required for teachers who need it. Removal with dignity must take place for those very few teachers for whom remediation is not effective.

7. The most critical professional performance of a teacher is daily teaching. Other professional behaviors involve establishing productive relationships outside the classroom with staff members, administrators, parents, and community members. A professional's responsibility for self-diagnosis and continuing growth is involved in all of the above.

8. The purpose of peer coaching or supervision is to provide a formative process with increasing professional effectiveness and artistry as the result. Such formative evaluation should occur early enough so teachers can benefit from it during the school year.

9. The purpose of a district's specified evaluation is summative, based on a year's professional performance, and certifies (with adequate sampling and data) a professional as belonging to a category that can range from outstanding to unacceptable. Summative evaluation is extremely important but, in terms of time requirement, is a small part of the process of staff development. It becomes the final assessment of the district's and teacher's efforts.

10. Summative evaluation is fair and just if, and only if, it has three qualities. First, it is based on many performance samples (not on one observation or on hearsay). Second, summative evaluation should be conducted only by an adequately trained evaluator. Last, summative evaluation should be based on stipulated criteria with meanings common to teacher and evaluator. This evaluative action should take into account that there are no absolutes

in teaching. Consequently, the presence or absence of any teaching or student behavior is not a definite indicator of effectiveness. Rather, summative evaluation should reflect the situational appropriateness and artistry of teacher behaviors that have been observed.

11. Competent evaluators must demonstrate expertise in two key areas if they are going to conduct valid teacher appraisals. Before evaluators enter the classroom, they must possess knowledge of the research-based, cause-effect relationships between teaching and learning. This involves knowing the difference between correlates of effective teaching and casual relationships between teaching and learning.

After demonstrating a knowledge of research-based, cause-effect relationships, evaluators must demonstrate competence in observation and conferencing skills. They need to be able to script tape an episode of teaching, recording objective data of teacher-learner behaviors. After script taping a teaching episode, the script tape should be analyzed to identify and label teaching behaviors that have a high probability of increasing or interfering with student learning. Using the script tape analysis, the evaluator must then generate an appropriate conference objective and plan for a growth-evoking conference. While conducting that conference, the evaluator needs to be able to make "on the spot" modifications in the conference plan based on the teacher's needs and responses.

After the classroom observation and subsequent conference, the evaluator should evaluate the meeting and infer reasons for success or lack of success in the teacher's professional growth. Additionally, the evaluator should use information derived from the conference to improve the effectiveness of subsequent interactions with the teacher.

The typical overburdened school administrator may argue, "There is not enough time to do a quality job of evaluation," or "I'm too busy putting out fires to do what is indicated in valid supervision and evaluation," or "Teachers want to be left alone to teach, not be pushed into increasingly effective teaching." We do, however, have evidence that translating these assumptions into reality is not only possible within a normal school day, but that translation is essential to the future of schooling.

Procedures for Translating Assumptions into Reality

To make these basic assumptions about teacher evaluation a reality, a continuing staff development program must be installed. This program for teachers, coaches, supervisors, and principals should produce an articulated, research-based, consistent, and conceptually coherent set of generalizations about effective teaching (including the notion that "there are no absolutes in teaching"). These generalizations must be in a language that has common meaning for teachers and evaluators. Teachers, coaches, supervisors, and evaluators must be given in-depth and continuous training to move them through the stages of learning, from propositional or declarative knowledge (generalizations about learning) to procedural knowledge (how it is done in practice), and, finally, into conditional knowledge (when and why each proposition is appropriate). At the conditional knowledge level, teachers, coaches, supervisors, and principals should know when and why each proposition is appropriate. During this continuous staff development program, frequent observations and appropriate feedback will keep staff members progressing toward sophisticated conditional knowledge and artistry in their practice.

Prerequisites for Valid Teacher Evaluation

There are several prerequisites to achieving this nirvana of teacher evaluation.

First, a long-range, research-based, conceptually coherent staff development program must be mounted in the district or individual school. This program becomes the philosophical and psychological base for staff development. (A long-range, conceptually coherent staff development program does not consist of occasional inservice sessions that take a patchwork quilt approach with unrelated topics or "the latest" in workshops.) An example of an appropriate philosophic statement might be, "All students can learn; their variance exists in the time necessary to accomplish that learning." From this statement a staff development program can be derived to teach skills of task analysis, diagnosis, prescription, learning styles, setting appropriate objectives, and using psychological principles related to accelerating learning. In such a program, learning "questioning skills" or "accommodating learning styles" becomes an integrated part of a professional mantle rather than a patchwork of skills.

Second, adequate leadership as a major professional assignment must be provided for a staff development program. We have ample evidence that staff development doesn't just happen. Only with designated leadership responsibilities will it be planned, supported, implemented, and evaluated. The result should be steady escalation of professional skills in teaching, coaching, supervising, and evaluating.

Third, adequate resources of time and money must be provided rather than depending on the charity of teachers' dedication, commitment, and spare time. Some of the greatest learning dividends from the tax dollar accrue from investment in increased professional competence.

Fourth, there is no point in administrators lamenting that "these skills should have been acquired in pre-service education." Frequently they are not. We can't reverse time, but we can develop more effective programs for current teacher preparation. Also, no matter how well prepared the beginning teacher is, new insights and techniques continue to emerge from research. Those contributions to professional proficiency need to be systematically acquired by teachers in the field.

Fifth, an evaluation program that measures results from staff development in terms of performance behavior, rather than paper and pencil knowledge, needs to be developed. Validation of success plus productive modifications of the program must be suggested and supported by data, not wishful thinking.

Sixth, teachers must have the inservice, coaching, and time necessary (much more than we formerly realized or currently allow) to acquire new skills and translate them into effective and artistic classroom practice. It is naive to teach questioning skills on Tuesday afternoon and expect to see them proficiently practiced on Wednesday morning (or even a month from Wednesday morning).

Seventh, proficiency occurs when skilled coaching or supervision are available as teachers practice new skills in their classrooms. Note the word is coaching, not tutoring, which implies a one-to-one relationship. Effective coaching can occur in groups, with the additional dividend of observational learning by all group members. It is not true that you must always do something to learn it. You must only do something to validate that you have learned it. All of us have had the experience of turning a class over to a student and watching a clone of ourselves teach. The student has learned our words ("show me you are ready to be dismissed") our mannerisms (a "look") and our techniques (walking around inspecting work) from observing us.

We have neglected this very powerful way of acquiring professional knowledge, skills, and procedures through observation of excellent practice, plus observation of the coaching that helps one achieve it. Seminar sessions using videotapes of effective teaching, and eventually the videotaped lesson of one of the participants, can become an efficient, effective, and low-cost method for a great deal of peer coaching and supervision.

Peer coaches are not assumed to be as proficient as highly trained observers. Nonetheless, peer coaching, supervision, and evaluation all require the same knowledge about cause-effect relationships between teaching and learning, the same ability to recognize appropriate use of those relationships in practice, and the same ability to script tape, analyze, and give growth-evoking feedback. (An evaluator has the additional responsibility of assigning the teacher to a category that can determine the teacher's future status: satisfactory, recommended for tenure, outstanding, needs remediation.)

Qualities Necessary for Coaching, Supervising, and Evaluating

Excellence in teaching results from implementation of knowledge of content, awareness of and response to different learning preferences and styles, and skills in pedagogy (the art and science of teaching that makes learning more predictably achievable).

Content, of course, varies from subject to subject. Clearly, an observer unfamiliar with the content being taught can be of little help in the teacher's content decisions. Knowledge of learning styles and pedagogy, on the other hand, is universal. The principles of learning are valid regardless of content, organizational scheme, age, or ethnic derivation of the learner. Tailoring learning styles and principles of learning is done to meet individual learning requirements.

Content. Content can be an academic discipline; a cognitive process such as thinking, writing, or discussing; an affective process such as appreciating, feeling, empathizing; or a psychomotor process such as playing ball, playing an instrument, or handwriting.

In the category of content, a process instructional objective is focused on learning how to do that process vs. using that process to accomplish a learning (learning to read vs. reading to learn).

The observer needs to ask the following questions about content.

1. Is the content in line with the district curriculum and expectations?

2. Are key concepts, generalizations, and discriminations essential to that content being taught, or are students being prepared for "trivial pursuits"?

3. Are students demonstrating by their achievement (with effort) that the level of difficulty is appropriate? Is the content "over their heads" or "under their feet?" Is a step essential for their achievement being omitted?

4. Is the sequence of content moving toward a perceivable objective, or are the time and energy of both teachers and students being deflected or consumed by extraneous matters that appear to be related?

Learning Behavior. The observer needs to ask the following questions about what the student is doing to learn (input) and to show he or she has learned (output).

1. Are students' learning activities appropriate to what is supposed to be learned? (Are students working together to learn how to cooperate or are they only memorizing rules about cooperation?)

2. Would a multimodality approach be appropriate to or interfere with the content objective and learner? Is the teacher obtaining perceivable evidence that validates students' learning? Is the teacher modifying instruction on the basis of that evidence when change of input or output behaviors are indicated?

Teacher Behavior. The observer needs to ask a number of questions to determine if the teacher is effectively using principles of learning. It is not the number of principles being employed, but the appropriateness and artistry of their use that constitutes effective teaching.

1. Are students putting forth effort to learn? If not, is the teacher employing principles of motivation to stimulate that effort? Or is the teacher wasting time "motivating" already motivated students?

2. Which principles is the teacher employing appropriately to increase the rate and degree of learning?

3. Which principles of learning is the teacher appropriately using to make retention of what is being learned more probable?

4. Is the teacher appropriately using principles of transfer to accelerate learning and increase the probability that the learning will transfer accurately to new situations requiring problem solving, creativity, and responsible decision making?

A District Staff Development and Teacher Evaluation Program

With all of this preamble to a successful and acceptable teacher evaluation program for Elm Hills School District, let's look at the process of mounting such a program. Granted, some of these steps may need to be telescoped, omitted, or augmented for political (not educational) reasons.

The district begins by creating a staff development and evaluation plan with a group of administrators and key teachers. This should produce (1) a purposeful and orderly two- to five-year plan rooted in reality and (2) identification of necessary resources of time and money that need to be budgeted. If these resources are not available, objectives are scaled down or timelines extended. Think big but realistically is the motto. It is at this phase of planning that district philosophy is articulated and alignment of staff development activities to that philosophy and resulting policy is validated. Except in an emergency, no ad hoc diversions of resources should be allowed. Modifications in the plan should be made only on the basis of emerging wisdom.

The staff development program should begin small, resisting the temptation to serve everyone. A pilot project that includes administrators, and possibly excellent teachers, can fix snags in the program before they pollute a larger group.

In formulating the plan for staff development, five critical elements need to be considered.

1. Administrators must be trained from the beginning. In most cases, they will be responsible for the end product of evaluation. Administrators learn cause-effect teaching relationships more slowly because a substantial part of their time is spent on administrative rather than teaching-learning matters. Teachers, on the other hand, spend more than five hours each day addressing the cause-effect relationship between teaching and learning. With more practice, teachers learn faster.

2. Because teachers have more classroom opportunities to learn, there

is a temptation for administrators to "turn staff development over to the teachers" under the guise of "democratic governance." Administrators then return to their former security, albeit ineffectual: the effectiveness of misapplied evaluative checklists.

3. To hold teachers responsible for skills they haven't had an opportunity to learn or to use psychological terms with which teachers are not familiar violates what teachers are held accountable for doing with students. Furthermore, coaches, supervisors, and evaluators should model the very best in the practice of teaching and in the evaluation of the success of that teaching. Teachers in the staff development program should experience the effectiveness of excellent instruction by participating in the staff development program.

4. Teaching, coaching, supervising, and evaluating are performance behaviors that are not learned overnight. One does not learn to be a musician, artist, athlete, surgeon, or pilot from just knowing what to do. One must learn simpler skills before more complex ones and should practice until each is synthesized into a high-speed, automatic, artistic performance. A teacher, of course, must develop skill in complex, high-speed decision making to immediately process and respond to all the subtle student cues emerging during the teaching-learning performance.

5. Education is a profession where one is continually adding to and refining knowledge that is not operative until it is translated, through practice, into increasingly skilled and artistic performance. The typical bright educator works on any technique about two years before it becomes automatic and artistic. This does not mean that we can't begin using that technique tomorrow morning, but it means that we should hold reasonable expectations for others (and ourselves) when asking for a change in teacher behavior. To think about teacher evaluation without keeping all of these assumptions, procedures, and cautions clearly in mind leads to a superficial or robotic checklist evaluation system.

Teacher Evaluation in Action

How would a defensible teacher evaluation system look in action? First, you would see 50 to 100 hours of training for evaluators in the process of instruction. This must come before training in coaching, supervision, and evaluation. The superintendent of Elm Hills School District may plead, "We don't have that much time," but the current problem in teacher evaluation is the result of such thinking. By the most conservative estimate, it takes approximately 50 hours for coaches, supervisors, and evaluators to learn some (by no means all) of the propositions related to cause-effect relationships between teaching and learning. Let's take, for example, one such proposition: "Mass practice for fast learning. Distribute practice for long retention."

First, evaluators will need practice identifying this proposition in video or live segments of teaching, pre-selected to highlight appropriate or inappropriate use of the proposition. Also, evaluators need to practice incorporating this proposition in their own teaching of students and adults, making prior and on-the-spot informed judgments about appropriateness or inappropriateness of each teacher or student behavior. Teaching a small group of students for several days or planning and conducting a staff meeting that requires massed or distributed practice will reveal internalization of effective teaching skills.

All of these 50 to 100 hours of training, reinforcement, refinement, and correction should be provided by a skilled trainer. While it is possible to do a "boot-strap" operation, it also can be highly fallible and ineffective. Self-instruction in beginning performance behavior is not recommended in surgery, athletics, music, or teacher evaluation. Outside assistance is typically needed.

The next stage of training in coaching, supervising, and evaluating focuses on observation and analysis skills. Beginning with pre-selected videotapes, participants first see how exemplary teaching practices look in excellent daily teaching practice. Next, the skill of script taping must be learned. A script tape is an anecdotal record of what is happening during a segment of teaching. That script tape becomes the diagnostic instrument from which professional growth is reinforced or prescribed. It takes about two hours of practice on five-minute teaching segments for most people to learn to script tape. It takes continuing practice to automate it for use in observation. There is no one best way to script tape. Each person develops abbreviations that are meaningful so a reasonably verbatim account of what went on can be read back with the temporal relationships of cause and effect supported. Because temporal relationships are critical to teaching and learning, boxes or checklists for recording are useless in observations.

A script tape provides a record flexible enough to accommodate any teaching style or instructional mode. If discovery is the mode, the observer script tapes the actions or discussions or experiments. If cooperative learning is the mode, the script tape records what is going on in the cooperative learning group.

The most time-consuming aspect of learning to use script taping is the subsequent analysis and psychological labeling of what occurred in the teaching segment, which requires professional judgment of appropriateness and artistry as well as identifying behaviors about which the observer has questions. (A conclusion about inappropriateness can't be drawn until the observer learns why the teacher chose a particular action.)

Two lists of behaviors are derived from a script tape: those behaviors that contributed to learning and those that had potential for interfering with learning. These lists provide the data from which content for the conference is selected.

The observer eliminates many teaching behaviors and selects for the focus of the conference a few behaviors with the greatest growth potential. The observer must understand that the focus of the conference may need to be modified or changed as data emerge during the conference.

Fifty to 100 hours of training under the tutelage of a competent trainer are needed to develop skill in script tape analyzing and conferencing. This time is the basic foundation for valid teacher evaluation. The power of any system of evaluation lies in the coaching and supervisory phase when there is the potential to reinforce, remediate, and stimulate professional growth. At the time of the summative evaluation, it is too late to make a difference. That final evaluation, however, may ready teachers for future coaching or supervision.

To stimulate professional growth, an increasingly difficult set of skills must be acquired by coaches, supervisors, and evaluators to conduct a growth-evoking teacher conference. All of the skills necessary for effective teaching must be in place plus the ability to encourage a practicing professional to pursue further growth.

In a formative conference, there are five potential messages. The coach or supervisor can use a "mix or match" strategy, depending on the primary objective of the interaction.

1. "Your teaching contributed to student learning when _____." The observer, using the script tape, describes what the teacher did that had high probability of resulting in a learning outcome, labeling the teacher's action with its psychological name ("mass practice"), to build common language and clarify the conditions that suggest a particular teaching behavior was a productive choice.

2. "Your procedure worked beautifully. If in another situation it doesn't work, what are some other things you might do?" "Some other ideas might be _____." This conference technique equips teachers with alternatives for future situations.

3. "What went just the way you anticipated it would?" "Were there any surprises?" "Would you make any changes in future lessons?" Phrasing questions carefully avoids implying that something was wrong and encourages teachers to analyze their own lessons. Teachers need, however, to have a certain degree of professional sophistication before they will be able to analyze their own teaching behaviors.

4. "What was your thinking when you _____?" This can reveal the reasons for an action that the observer perceived as unproductive. In some instances, asking such a question helps the observer better understand the teacher's decisions. Having a clearer picture can enable the observer to offer suggestions or alternatives for the teacher to try.

5. "You are a very skilled teacher, what would you like to work on next

to add to your professional competence?" This message acknowledges competence and emphasizes that professional growth never stops.

It is important to remember that the focus of every conference is on the future. The observed lessons will never be taught again to those students. The script tape provides diagnostic evidence of what the teacher needs to learn to implement new skills and enhance or remediate old ones. In coaching and supervision, the objective of the conference is to add insights rather than make judgments.

Only in a summative conference is the teacher placed in a category that results from a "sum" of all evidence gathered from observations and from other relevant aspects of the teacher's assignment during the year.

During the initial stages of learning how to script tape and conference, simulated conferences are planned and conducted from script tapes of videotaped lessons. Eventually, teachers who have strong egos plus skills in helping a coach, supervisor, or evaluator grow should be recruited to be "guinea-pigs." Potential coaches, supervisors, and evaluators can observe, script tape, and conference these teachers.

Only after such trial runs are participants ready to be turned loose on real, day-to-day teaching. They will need, however, to continue to develop skills for the rest of their professional lives. Remember, the power of an actual instructional conference is so great that, like surgery, it should not be conducted until skills are established and validated in simulation.

Periodic refresher courses for coaches, supervisors, and evaluators must be planned and scheduled to eliminate undesirable mutations that inevitably occur in any program and to build in the robustness of new research-based information as it emerges. Achieving professional competence and evaluative excellence is a never-ending endeavor.

None of the above is accomplished by wishful thinking, but is the result of a rigorous program designed to develop and validate possession of the necessary skills. Only through this long path of training can valid teacher evaluation become a reality.

Sequence of Activities in the School Year

Assuming all of the ingredients of a defensible staff development and teacher evaluation program are in place, let's look at the sequence of a school year that culminates in successful evaluation and satisfied, growing teachers. This means that teachers have been evaluated on criteria that they have had the opportunity to learn and that research indicates have high impact on students' learning, as well as on their professional performance outside the classrooms.

Telling Teachers About Teacher Evaluation

At the beginning of the school year, a general district or local school staff meeting should be held to explain coaching, supervision, and evaluation procedures and the staff development program that will make these procedures successful. Teachers will hear that all observations during the year, whether by peer coaches, supervisors, or principals, are for the purpose of continual enhancement of their own teaching effectiveness. At the end of the year, there will be a formal, written evaluation based on how much each teacher has grown in professional skills during the year and the skill with which the teacher now teaches as a result of the year's coaching and supervision.

Teachers need to know that they will be observed, routinely and frequently, for short periods of time and that the observer will script tape during each observation, even if the visit is only a few minutes. Script taping should be demonstrated so teachers can see what it is and why it is useful.

Districtwide Staff Development Plan

If inservice sessions have not been initiated, they should be held before the implementation of any teacher evaluation model because teachers first need to learn the cause-effect relations between teaching and learning. It is strongly advised that teachers understand the three categories of teaching decisions (content, learner behavior, and teacher behavior) plus motivation, reinforcement, and practice theory before "lesson design" is introduced.

Many principals and staff development trainers want to begin with lesson design because it is so practical. To do so is an error because teachers do not know the theory from which lesson design was derived. Consequently, lesson design may be erroneously perceived as a "recipe" for what the classroom observer expects to see rather than a series of decisions made by the teacher about what to include or exclude in a particular lesson.

As each of the fundamentals of teaching decisions (motivation, reinforcement, practice, and lesson design) are learned, teachers can practice translating knowledge into their classroom. As they do, subsequent inservice sessions should add other cause-effect relationships to teachers' repertoires so the staff development program is a dynamic process of escalating competence, not a static model of "what to do."

Schoolwide Staff Development Plan

Building principals should promote staff growth in their schools. For example, during staff meetings, two- to three-minute videotaped segments of teaching by an unknown teacher can be shown to staff members while the principal script tapes what is happening during the episode. The script tape should be read back to the staff members so they see the script tape as a running anecdotal record of what was happening during the period of observation and not just a recording of teaching errors.

Teachers should be encouraged to learn script taping themselves so they become aware of the power such an approach brings to discussions about teaching. Remember, script taping provides a record of what actually happened so an observer doesn't have to rely on vague and sometimes faulty recollections. If a quality program of peer coaching is to be in place at a school, teachers must learn to script tape and label the teaching behaviors of their colleagues.

Moreover, a schoolwide staff development plan encourages observational learning. Teachers can learn much about instruction by actually observing teachers in action or watching first-rate instructional practices exemplified in videotape segments. Seeing the cause-effect relationships between what a teacher does and how much students learn is a powerful learning tool.

From these short video episodes, both principals and teachers can learn to recognize and analyze effective teaching and learning behaviors. Principals and teachers should work together to identify the conditions that suggest a particular teaching behavior would have been effective. Using a videotape as an instructional tool can help clarify when a particular technique should and should not be used. Remember, there are no absolutes in teaching, and teachers need to develop tolerance for this ambiguity so they make conscious and informed decisions rather than "doing what you're supposed to do."

Conferencing with Teachers

At the beginning of the year, the question of a pre-observational conference should be addressed. If a quality teacher evaluation and staff development plan are in place, there is little need for a pre-observational conference. If the teacher has been working on a particular skill or technique, the principal should already know about it as a result of staff meetings and previous observations. Should the teacher wish the principal to take particular note of anything, a quick oral or written request should suffice, but this can hardly be called a pre-observation conference. If the teacher is convinced the principal will not know what is going on unless told beforehand, re-education of one of the two is indicated.

Pre-observational conferences can generate three problems.

1. The observer comes to observation with a bias of what will occur. Prior expectations have been shown to distort observation of what actually occurred.

2. Having told the principal what will happen pressures teachers to see that it happens even when it shouldn't.

3. Pre-conferences take time and energy to schedule and conduct, consuming two of the most scarce resources in the school.

Except in rare cases, pre-observational conferences are unnecessary. Mandated pre-observational conferences are a holdover from days when the only way untrained principals knew what was going on was to be told in advance. Teachers should know that they will be given carefully considered feedback during a post-observation conference. (A brief hall encounter with the principal saying, "You were doing a great job," with no specifics of why it was great and consequently no opportunity to grow in professional knowledge and practice, is unacceptable.) Conferences should be scheduled after any classroom observation of more than a brief duration.

Teachers encountering difficulty with instruction have a right to specific recommendations for improvement. During subsequent observations, they should be given appropriate feedback and reinforcement so that increasingly effective professional skills can be acquired.

The typical post-observation conference takes from 10 to 30 minutes. If the purpose of the conference is to plan the next lesson, however, more time may be needed because the teacher and principal will need to think their way through the labyrinth of task analysis and lesson design. (In this case, the principal takes joint ownership of the subsequent classroom learning results, and both professionals grow in the process.)

Only after teachers begin to understand the observation-conference process are they ready to be observed.

Uncertainty and a certain amount of defensiveness are normal reactions to the new experience of an observation whose purpose is growth-evoking rather than judgmental. Teachers may need many observation and conference experiences to be comfortable with this procedure.

Classroom Observations

There is a lot of useless debate over whether observations should be announced or unannounced. It makes little difference except in opportunity for preparation. Effective teachers are not going to teach poorly because they didn't expect to be observed. An ineffective teacher will not magically develop preparation and teaching skills the night before the observation and often brings in more prepared materials (junk) than is needed for the lesson. Usually it is wise to let teachers decide whether they prefer scheduled or unannounced visits. Because there will be both scheduled and drop-in observations, the principal needs to let staff members know there will be many visits in each classroom. Teacher and students will soon become accustomed to another professional's presence in the room and, as a result, classwork won't be interrupted. Teachers should be assured that the principal does not expect to be openly acknowledged.

A few teachers may avoid being observed by turning the class over to the visitor. ("Boys and girls, we're always happy to have

_____ as a visitor in our classroom. This is an opportunity for you to tell what we have been doing or to ask any question you wish.") The first time this "class dumping" occurs, the observer should gracefully accept the limelight and later explain to the teacher that the class should proceed as if a visitor were not present. If this does not eliminate the problem, the observer should graciously turn the class back to the teacher, sit down, and observe so "class dumping" is not reinforced. Again, there are no absolutes because there are times when a visitor becomes a needed resource and can assist with student learning activities.

After each visit, teachers should receive some positive feedback from the observer that reinforces an appropriately used instructional strategy. For example, a principal might say, "Mrs. Jones, when you asked students to give an example of when they might use multiplication in their own lives, you were making the process really meaningful to them and giving them reasons to develop facility with their multiplication facts."

If during a brief visit the observer notes a teacher action that appears to interfere with students' learning, it is wise to observe again to see if the behavior is typical or was a one-time occurrence. If the behavior seems to be typical, the teacher's reasons for that behavior should be determined before it is judged inappropriate.

Remember, however, that teachers need to be taught the principles of learning before they are expected to exhibit them in the classroom. Teachers, like students, should be given appropriate feedback so they may consciously and deliberately use those principles in future teaching. If something did not go well during the observed teaching, the observer must be able to provide the teacher with a potentially more effective behavior. Effective feedback can only be accomplished if the coach or supervisor knows principles of learning, recognizes the absence or presence of them in the classroom, and can model them while coaching, supervising, and evaluating teachers.

When observing teachers, principals need to keep in mind the need for both massed and distributed practice because long retention of exemplary teaching strategies is the goal. Consequently, the principal should observe a few teachers 3 or 4 times for 10 to 20 minutes within a 2- to 3-week period. This provides the massed practice necessary for teachers to learn quickly and also tells the principal if supervision resulted in increased excellence in teaching. Then those teachers may not be observed, except for brief drop-ins, for several weeks while the principal is observing other teachers. After a few weeks, when the first group of teachers has had a chance to develop beginning automaticity and artistry, the principal returns to them to observe for distributed practice that produces long retention of some exemplary skills, or for more massed practice to introduce new skills.

The district-negotiated agreement on classroom observations must be met. It is just as important, however, to individualize supervisory instruction for teachers as it is to individualize classroom instruction for students. Some teachers profit from continuing frequent observations; some need longer spaces between observations to work out their own ways of "accommodation and assimilation" of new or refined teaching decisions and behaviors. Once teachers begin to savor the growth potential of a collaborative supervisory relationship, the effective observer will never have enough time to meet observation requests.

Record Keeping

At a staff meeting at the beginning of the year, the matter of keeping records needs to be addressed. The script tape is a nonjudgmental record of what happened during a particular teaching episode. At the subsequent conference, the principal has a number of options regarding the script tape. Some summary notes may be made and the script tape can be given to the teacher. If the principal must have a record of when and what was observed, the teacher can have a copy of the script tape. Except in the very rare occasion of a dismissal case, the script tape does not become a part of personnel records but is kept to remind the principal of points for future observations.

A great deal of time and effort is often directed to the final summary evaluation. The critical portion of evaluation is the authenticity of the data summarized. Should the data be causal of student learning, a summary sheet that records "most of the time," "some of the time," and "never" is relevant. Should the evaluation summary note only the presence or absence of teaching behaviors that correlate with effective teaching, but may or not have been appropriate in a specific lesson, then that evaluation summary is of no relevance to professional excellence.

All observation or evaluation criteria that list specific behaviors should have the qualifier "if/as appropriate." This, of course, requires judgment (with the necessary evidence) on the part of the observer. Quality training with performance certification by a competent trainer is the only way to guarantee an observer's accurate and professional judgment.

Inclusion of Paraprofessionals

A decision needs to be made about when aides or volunteers are to be included in staff development meetings. Some teachers prefer that they have a running start on teaching effectiveness so they can help transmit effective practice to aides and volunteers. Other teachers want their paraprofessionals with them in the same staff development meetings. In either case, it is essential that there be a planned program for aides and volunteers, not a "hope" that training will be done by teachers, who may be unable or too busy to contribute to the achievement of competence by paraprofessionals.

Preparation of Evaluators

Next, the task is to translate the professional-growth-evoking, coaching, supervision, and evaluation program into reality. This requires two ingredients. The first is a well-planned staff development program collaboratively designed by all people affected so it has a research-based, continuing focus where each skill or decision being learned relates to previous skills and leads to future competence. This is a far cry from the "What will we focus on for this inservice meeting?" or "Whom can we get to speak?" patchwork of most staff meetings. Even worse is the staff meeting with a focus on administrative trivia that would have been better handled by a bulletin teachers could read and use as needed.

The second essential ingredient for a successful program is a principal who is committed to the notion that increasing instructional effectiveness is the number one goal for schools. The principal's skill in planning and implementing staff development and supervision is the best predictor of whether this goal will be met. The principal also needs to take responsibility for and advantage of opportunities for continuing self-renewal and professional growth and, as a result, be a model for staff members. Principals who practice what they preach set the tone for professional excellence in the school. Granted, the principal has other important demands on time. Granted, there is never enough time for adequate supervision. But as the principal develops supervisory skills, more can be accomplished in less time. (This also is true in the classroom.) Principals should set aside an absolute minimum of 2 hours a week for both walk through and 10- to 20-minute classroom observations (with subsequent brief conferences). These well-spent hours can guarantee dividends by reducing the number of student problems and parent concerns. A reduction in problems and concerns will eventually yield additional time that can be used for staff development and supervision. Alerting parents to the school's staff development program will elicit their support. (These same principles can be shared with parents to help them increase their parenting effectiveness.)

Next, we need to deal with the argument that the supervisor should not also be the evaluator. The reasons given, which we consider invalid, are (1) teachers will not reveal needs or weakness to someone who eventually will pass judgment on professional effectiveness and (2) the evaluator will bias subsequent evaluation on the basis of previous problems whether or not they have been resolved.

Our argument against both of these statements is (1) weakness in teaching cannot be concealed from a competent evaluator and (2) subsequent evaluation will be biased in favor of teachers who have the maturity to accurately assess themselves and request help to remediate weakness. To argue that not all evaluators are nonbiased and competent is to argue that because this may be the current state, it is all right for the biased and incompetent to evaluate teachers.

Timeline for Coaching, Supervision, and Evaluation

During the first two weeks of school in the fall, the principal should be highly visible in "walk throughs" in classrooms. This habituates students and teachers to the principal's presence and gives the principal valid diagnostic data of teaching skills that are already present and what needs to be learned. It also has a reassuring effect on parents when they hear, "The principal was in our room today!"

Giving teachers informal positive feedback from those brief observations reassures them that the principal is looking for what is right rather than what is wrong.

Even though the principal should have a tentative, school-based staff development program in mind before school starts, diagnostic data from these beginning brief observations may modify the plan. Usually a staff development committee has been created to form and re-form the year's staff development plans. Although "ownership" is the current descriptor for such an approach, it is not ownership that sells the program but the teacher's positive feelings and perceptions that develop as a result of professional growth.

Once the beginning school adjustments are made and inevitable snarls unraveled, systematic, growth-evoking supervision begins. It is advantageous to start with the most expert teachers. It takes little to stimulate them to continuing growth, and the rest of the staff then bonds supervision to effectiveness rather than remediation. Those teachers also are potential future coaches who can augment, not replace, the principal's efforts.

When feedback conferences with those excellent teachers are helpful, the word spreads and the principal winds up with more requests for observations than can be scheduled. As a principal, it's often tempting to work only with "those teachers who want to learn." The teacher faces the same problem with students in a classroom. But like the teacher, the principal must provide learning opportunities for the less aggressive, reluctant, or remedial staff learners. Giving these teachers a choice of "this week or would you rather wait until next week?" makes it clear that an observation will occur but leaves them in charge of when.

Should a teacher be in serious trouble, the principal or other competent supervisory help needs to be immediately available. In this case, observations of other teachers may have to wait. Working with an instructional difficulty as soon as it surfaces saves hours of time later. An exception to this generalization is the mediocre teacher who has barely stayed afloat for years. A week or two of help will not solve this situation, so it is better to work first with stronger staff members thereby freeing the time necessary to accomplish the difficult feat of changing long-practiced, inappropriate teaching behaviors.

After the initial six weeks to two months of supervision, which has been a combination of walk through and longer observation, the principal needs to take stock of what has been accomplished. Unless reasonable results are perceivable, modification is needed.

By the beginning of the third month of school, observations and conferences should be a routine of concentrating on a manageable group of teachers for two to four weeks, then changing focus to a new group of teachers with only occasional visits to the first group to maintain quality practice and to stimulate new growth. Eventually, observations will rotate back to each group for additional distributed practice.

The principal and staff members need to judge when it will be possible and desirable to free the teachers who have been trained to observe and give feedback to work with their colleagues. If the school has budgeted for it, substitutes can be hired to free teachers for observations and conferences.

Probably the most efficient and effective observational learning occurs when teachers videotape their own lessons. After viewing the lesson, the teacher can decide to erase the video or let colleagues view and discuss it. Allowing colleagues to view a videotaped lesson results in growth for the entire group as they discuss the cause and effect relationships observed. If paraprofessionals are included in these staff development sessions, acceleration of their skills, a new respect for the complexity of teaching, and the desire for continuing staff development are highly probable outcomes.

Videotaping and group viewing, however, usually will not occur during the first year of the program. If a staff development program is successfully mounted, effective teachers will routinely schedule growth-evoking "views" of their teaching during the second year. Some teachers may even volunteer lessons to be viewed by the entire staff for observational learning and discussion.

It is especially effective when principals take the lead in this growth process by videotaping themselves teaching students and then analyzing that tape for a group and inviting comments about situations where similar behaviors would be appropriate or inappropriate. Through this process, staff members will learn that no one is a perfect teacher and all teaching is "never as good as you hoped or as bad as you feared."

Throughout the year this staff development cycle of inservice, viewing tapes and working with colleagues, supervising observations and conferences helps teachers to:
- Learn relevant educational/psychological theory.
- Translate theory into practice.

- Determine the conditions under which the principles of learning are or are not appropriately applied.
- Reinforce (or remediate) teaching practices.
- Refine, extend, and develop artistry in teaching.

The sequence of these activities should be custom-tailored to the needs of each staff.

When the teacher evaluation program is in full bloom, almost all staff members will move toward growth in professional competence. Collegial collaboration can become established as an important educational function. Teachers will learn to collaborate in making decisions (rather than sharing dittos), and ongoing professional growth in curriculum and instruction will become an increasingly established procedure. Two important elements should be added to the program: (1) curricular competence in each discipline in terms of district articulated outcomes and (2) facility (artistry) in communication with parents. Each should be addressed in staff meetings, job-alike seminars, and teacher-principal conferences.

Summative Evaluation

Many principals see only the obligation of evaluation and not its potential for growth. Evaluation can be viewed as an unpleasant but necessary chore that accompanies leadership, but it can also be viewed as the springboard to professional effectiveness as the evaluator and teacher stimulate each other's continuing growth.

Having been heavily involved in all the above activities, the principal should be well equipped to summatively evaluate a teacher's performance at the time designated by district policy. There will be abundant objective data derived from that teacher's performance as a contributing member of the staff, the establishment of productive relationships with parents and community, an adherence to district policies and procedures, and continuing professional growth that is demonstrated in many samples of daily teaching. When a teacher receives an end-of-the-year evaluation based on broad evidence, rather than nonobjective impressions and one or two fateful observations, that evaluation is usually perceived as fair and accurate.

The criteria for evaluation must be appropriate to the professional skill and maturity of the teacher in the same way that learning objectives must be appropriate to the current performance of a student. Clearly, a beginning teacher is not expected to have the proficiency and artistry of an accomplished teacher. A less successful teacher should not be expected to attain exemplary professional competence after only one conference.

A final evaluation should have no surprises. All conclusions should be based on data previously discussed with the teacher and validated by script taped classroom evidence plus school professional performance, which is summarized in the final assessment.

Obviously, the most heavily weighted evidence of professional excellence comes from many observations of teaching. Where, you may ask, is the important factor of relationships with students, thereby building students' self-esteem? This factor is an integral part of the teaching process. Helping students be "right" rather than "catching them being wrong"; diagnosing so that, with effort, each student experiences success; disciplining students when necessary but always maintaining the "offender's" dignity; and developing in students a zest for learning are teaching skills that can be learned to a satisfactory level by most professionals. Possession of these skills, however, is validated through many observations.

The final evaluation of each teacher may be recorded on any form determined by the district. The objective evidence accrued in formative evaluations throughout the year should support a summative evaluation that includes the following categories:

I. Contributing member of a staff.

II. Implementor of district policies and procedures.

III. Effective communicator and participant with parents and community.

IV. Professionally growing teacher as evidenced by:

A. Curricular decisions in terms of district policy and content integrity.

B. Pedagogical competency in terms of:

1. Task analyzing content.

2. Diagnosing students' entry behavior and progress in that content.

3. Determining appropriate instructional objectives.

4. Designing and implementing effective lessons using, as appropriate, a variety of models of teaching and learning.

5. Monitoring students' learning while teaching.

6. Adjusting teaching on the basis of emerging data.

7. Appropriately applying principles that increase students' motivation, rate and degree of learning, retention, and transfer of that learning to creative problem solving and future decisions.

C. Continuing professional growth from staff development, observation, and conference experiences.

For any evaluation, there should be appeal procedures with each participant producing tangible evidence (script tape, number of observations, conference discussions, and conclusions) plus research-based, empirical support for the concerns. These data enable a teacher-appraisal team to determine "prejudice" or "informed conclusions." Remember, it is easier to help a poor teacher grow than to dismiss that teacher.

Conclusion

Teaching has grown from an occupation, to a craft, to a profession based on knowledge not commonly held outside of the field. Sophisticated peer coaching, supervision, and evaluation have the power to elevate teaching to the level of the very highest profession, for teachers work with the most complex part of the human: the brain. That brain, with its potential of 10 billion household computers, must be engaged in the production of proficient, responsible, and caring humans.

Teachers control the development of future leaders who will promote world peace, future physicians and researchers who will control disease, future scientists who will eliminate pollution and geographic destruction, future architects and engineers who will make our world beautiful and functional, future workers who will keep it all running economically and efficiently, and future teachers who make all other professions possible.

Surely with these goals in mind, we must not await, we must create a teacher coaching, supervision, and evaluation program that produces superb teachers who continue to increase in excellence throughout their professional lives.

Bibliography

Hunter, M. "Effecting a Reconciliation Between Supervision and Evaluation." *Journal of Personnel Evaluation* 1 (1988).

Hunter, M. *Mastery Teaching, Improved Instruction.* El Segundo, Calif.: TIP Publications, 1983.

Hunter, M. *Teach More—Faster.* El Segundo, Calif.: TIP Publications, 1976.

Hunter, M. *Retention.* El Segundo, Calif.: TIP Publications, 1967.

Hunter, M. *Transfer.* El Segundo, Calif.: TIP Publications, 1971.

MARCELLA VERDUN

From the Practitioner's Point of View...

For the past two years, my school has participated in a districtwide pilot project using the model Hunter describes. We've found a number of positive benefits.

In addition to improving teachers' instructional effectiveness, Hunter's model improves the proficiency of those who evaluate teachers.

The staff development component does indeed offer a common language that supervisors and teachers can use to discuss research-based concepts that can increase student learning—a language that helps establish bonds between teachers and supervisors. Discussions between teachers and evaluators are much more constructive when evaluators can skillfully analyze data for critical elements of instruction, and provide feedback in the form of reinforcement and remediation. The result is greater confidence for both parties, which facilitates growth.

We've also found that the recommended timelines for implementation are realistic.

Evaluation of this nature, as opposed to the more traditional judgmental checklists, offers added insights for both evaluators and teachers. Teachers now have more respect for the credibility of evaluators and the validity of supervision itself. And morale has improved.

Coincidental or not, our school has already experienced improvement in annual test scores since the inception of this program. We're convinced that our commitment and perseverance will result in long-lasting outcomes for students.

Marcella Verdun is Principal of Herman Elementary School in Detroit, Michigan. An educator for 20 years, Verdun has also served as a teacher, counselor, and assistant principal.

3 Judgment-Based Teacher Evaluation

W. JAMES POPHAM

UCLA Graduate School of Education
Los Angeles, California 90024

Dr. Harry Jergens
Superintendent
Elm Hills School District

Dear Dr. Jergens:

I was delighted that you asked me to serve as one of the external consultants who will be supplying you with advice regarding implementation of an effective, district-level teacher evaluation system.

Your request, I confess, forced me to organize my thinking about teacher evaluation. Off and on for almost 30 years, I've been wrestling with the problem of how to evaluate teachers. For the bulk of that period, I must concede, the problem has proved far more potent than this wrestler's skills.

In reality, teacher evaluation has been my own Moby Dick since the time I was a high school teacher. I trooped off to graduate school because, having encountered so many instances of ineffectual instruction in public schools, I wanted to do something to make teaching better.

W. James Popham is Professor, Department of Education, University of California, Los Angeles.

There are numerous teacher appraisal trails that researchers can travel. I've wandered down them all with a remarkable consistency of results—all dismal. But our public schools can't wait until teacher evaluation researchers solve all the technical problems surrounding teacher appraisal. As your situation in the Elm Hills School District vividly illustrates, we need sensible solution strategies now, not in another 30 years.

I hope you'll find the enclosed analysis useful. I am convinced that if America's school districts opt for a carefully developed judgment-based approach to teacher appraisal, we can make substantial strides in (1) providing skill-building support for the vast majority of our teachers and (2) successfully terminating that small number of incompetent teachers who are apt to be harming children.

Almost all current teacher evaluation systems are, at bottom, judgmentally based. We deceive ourselves if we pretend that formal data-gathering devices and statistical analyses cancel the necessity of relying on human judgment. The judgment-based approach to teacher evaluation, however, is designed to make such evaluative judgments more defensible.

I applaud your district for attempting to discharge a teacher you consider incompetent. Sadly, most district administrators and school boards do not have the courage to attempt such pupil-protection acts. In the accompanying essay, I have set forth the essentials of a teacher evaluation system that I believe you will find useful. In brief, I initially argue for a split between formative and summative teacher evaluation, then describe procedures for carrying out formative and summative teacher evaluation via a judgmentally based approach.

I hope you and your colleagues will find elements in the proposed scheme that will be of use in the Elm Hills School District.

Sincerely,

W. James Popham
Professor

A Defensible District-Level Teacher Appraisal Program

Creating an effective teacher evaluation system is costly. It requires dexterity, diligence, and dollars. Ineffective teacher evaluation systems, however, are even more costly. Shoddy teacher appraisal programs, because they neither improve teachers' instructional skills nor permit the dismissal of incompetent teachers, rob children of the achievements that, when well-taught, they have the potential to attain.

School-district officials must recognize that it takes a significant investment of energy and perhaps some additional funds to create a district-level teacher evaluation system that is more than rhetoric and ritual. School administrators who set out to install a meaningful teacher appraisal program must make a major commitment to developing a teacher evaluation system that truly makes a difference.

In this analysis I discuss a number of points that local school officials should consider when they adopt a new teacher evaluation system. If the procedures I recommend are adopted, then the district's teacher appraisal program is more apt to contribute to the major mission of American schools: promoting children's learning.

Formative and Summative Folly

Teacher evaluation in American education has two separate functions. The first centers on the improvement of teachers' skills so that they can perform their jobs more effectively. This type of teacher evaluation is frequently described as formative teacher evaluation, for its mission is to help modify (form) the teacher's instructional behaviors. There should be no tenure or termination decisions associated with formative teacher evaluation; it is exclusively improvement focused.

The second function of teacher evaluation centers on such decisions as whether to dismiss a teacher, whether to grant tenure to a teacher, whether to place a teacher on probation, or how much merit pay to give a teacher. This type of evaluation is typically called summative teacher evaluation because it deals with more final, summary decisions about teachers. Summative teacher evaluation is not improvement-oriented except in the sense that a school's instructional program is ultimately improved when an incompetent teacher is removed.

Formative and summative evaluation focus on fundamentally different tasks. From the perspective of teachers' unions, of course, formative teacher evaluation is far more palatable than summative because it threatens neither teacher jobs nor union dues. Summative teacher evaluation, on the other hand, can be used to send a teacher packing. It is, therefore, substantially more threatening.

In most school districts, formative and summative teacher evaluation are closely linked. Often these two functions are carried out by the same individual, typically a school's principal. Throughout the school year, the principal is usually obliged to provide teachers with suggestions for improvement as well as to make end-of-year judgments about the very same teachers.

In spite of its prevalence, the blending of formative and summative teacher evaluation represents a grave conceptual error. Both formative and summative evaluation are important functions, but these two teacher evaluation tasks must be carried out separately by different individuals (see also Stiggins 1986).

Consummate Contamination

Let's consider for a moment the essence of formative teacher evaluation, that is, the improvement of the teacher's skills. For improvement to occur, shortcomings must be identified. Ideally, a teacher and a formative evaluator should work together, perhaps in the context of some sort of clinical supervision model, to isolate elements of the teacher's instructional activities that need improvement. For example, if the teacher has difficulty in getting pupils to make smooth transitions from one activity to another, then the formative evaluation can focus on providing the teacher with strategies to improve between-activity transitions. Deficits, once identified, can be addressed.

But what if the teacher is unwilling to admit that deficits exist? How can a formatively oriented evaluator help fix something that, according to the teacher, doesn't need fixing? Therein, of course, lies the fundamental difficulty in trying to blend formative and summative teacher evaluation. If teachers believe that information gathered during formative evaluation will also be used to make a summative judgment against them, they will be reluctant to admit their shortcomings. Reluctance to parade one's weakness is a universal human trait.

Many administrators who have been thrust into the formative-summative evaluator role will protest that they can, having "earned the trust" of their teachers, carry out both teacher evaluation functions simultaneously. They are deluding themselves.

Recently, I presented to a group of teachers and administrators the proposal that formative and summative teacher evaluation be split. A panel of principals and then a panel of teachers reacted to my proposal. Although several of the principals allowed that it would be wonderful not to wear their formative and summative hats simultaneously, other principals argued that they established sufficient rapport with their teachers so that their formative function was not tainted by their summative responsibility. Twenty minutes later, the teacher panel unanimously conceded that the fear of negative summative appraisals drastically disinclined them to identify deficits during formative evaluation. Even though many principals believe that they can, via trust-inducing behavior, be both the helper-person and the hatchet-person, such beliefs are mistaken.

Function-Splitting

Compared to splitting the atom, separating formative from summative teacher evaluation should be fairly simple. Yet, because of education's long-standing meshing of these two functions, it isn't. There are three strategies district policymakers can use to separate the two functions. First, however, it is *essential* for the district's administrative leadership and governing board to strongly endorse a separation of the two teacher-evaluation functions. This endorsement should be officially authorized and widely publicized so that staff members and citizens know that there's a new approach to evaluation. Even with official approval, however, it will take some time for teachers to truly believe that formative information will *never* be used for summative appraisals. Only when this acceptance has finally occurred will the true potential of split-function teacher evaluation be realized. Thus, district officials must immediately install a never-to-be-violated policy that any information gathered by formative evaluators will never be shared with summative evaluators. Indeed, severe penalties should be involved if a formative evaluator ever breaches confidentiality by sharing with a summative evaluator any information gathered during formative evaluation.

Here are the three staffing options that district officials can consider when implementing a split-function teacher evaluation system.

Option One: Separation of Functions. If local schools have two administrators per site, assign formative and summative teacher evaluation functions to the different individuals. For example, the assistant principal could become the formative teacher-evaluator and the principal could become the summative teacher-evaluator, or vice versa. The division in responsibilities must, of course, be well publicized to staff members. The two administrators must never pool evaluative information. It may take time, of course, for teachers to believe that information collected during formative sessions is not be relayed to the summative evaluator. Both administrators must be trained in the particulars of the evaluation role that they are asked to fulfill. The costs of adopting this option, if the district is fortunate enough to have two or more administrators per school, are trivial.

Option Two: Teacher-Conducted Formative Evaluation. If school sites have only one administrator, promote the most instructionally astute teachers to become formative teacher evaluators. Such individuals would work full-time in formative teacher evaluation and, depending on staff sizes, could provide formative evaluation for teachers in several schools. This would allow a school's principal to function exclusively in a summative role. For if this option is to be successful, the teachers who assume the formative teacher-evaluator role must not be given an assistant principal's administrative chores. As with Option One, both formative and summative evaluators must be trained for their functions. The costs of this option are chiefly the costs of replacing the teachers who have become formative evaluators.

Option Three: District-Staffed Summative Evaluation. If there is only one administrator per site, make that administrator a formative evaluator. Summative evaluation would then fall to qualified and competent central office administrators. As before, both formative and summative evaluators must be well trained. Depending on the magnitude of the district's summative effort, the costs of this option could be fairly modest or rather substantial. Summative teacher evaluations, of course, are often carried out only biannually or triennially rather than annually, thus reducing the cost of such district-staffed evaluations.

Over the years, well-intentioned efforts to combine formative and summative teacher evaluation have created dysfunctional, counterproductive personnel appraisal schemes. We must let teachers and citizens know that we're going to separate those two important missions of teacher evaluation so that it will be possible to improve the skills of as many teachers as possible and to identify those teachers incapable of being improved so that they can be discharged.

Relative Importance of Formative and Summative Teacher Evaluation

In most states, there are statutory requirements to evaluate teachers summatively so that, if teachers are incompetent, they can be given remedial assistance and, if unremediable, dismissed. I completely support such requirements, for our first obligation in education should be to children, not teachers. However, on the basis of our current teacher appraisal technology, we typically find it difficult to conclude that a teacher should be discharged and make that conclusion stick if challenged. Thus, if educators are going to devise defensible evaluation systems, those systems must be carefully crafted. Summative teacher evaluation demands attention to detail (i.e., the procedural particulars of union contracts) and familiarity with the appropriateness of evidence of a teacher's proficiency.

Formative teacher evaluation, on the other hand, can help teachers grow in their skills. Better teachers will produce improved student achievement. Accordingly, we dare not undervalue the importance of formative teacher evaluation.

The remainder of this analysis addresses important features of both formative and summative teacher evaluation, with an emphasis on summative evaluation because most educators need help on that side of the ledger. But, to reiterate, both formative and summative teacher evaluation are significant functions that school districts must fulfill. Even if a district is required by state law to operate only a summative teacher evaluation program, district officials are responsible, by virtue of their profession and the ultimate well-being of children, to operate a formative program as well.

A Few Precepts for Formative Teacher Evaluators

I have only three suggestions for district officials who are already familiar with clinical supervision models or similar approaches for boosting teacher skills. If, of course, the district's leadership is not conversant with such improvement-focused schemes, then an all-out effort should be made to see that the district's administrative personnel become competent in the essentials of instructional supervision. It is nearly impossible to pick up an issue of *Educational Leadership*, for example, without being barraged by a number of articles focused on improving the quality of teaching.

Change the Name of the Game

My initial suggestion for a formative program deals with the phrase "formative teacher evaluation." It is true that roses, even if named otherwise, would smell as sweet. However, in the case of formative teacher evaluation, the name can be to blame. Whenever someone faces the prospect of being evaluated, there is the possibility of being found wanting. Most human beings, therefore, react negatively to the idea of being evaluated. Teachers are no different. Even if district officials underscore the adjective "formative" in all written documents, as well as raise their decibel level several notches when uttering the word, the adjective is nonetheless followed by a noun, namely, *evaluation*.

Although there may be technical dividends from distinguishing between formative and summative evaluation in analyses such as this, in day-to-day practice there is little profit to be garnered from using the phrase "formative evaluation." It conjures up too many teacher-threatening images. I strongly recommend that district administrators dump the negative connotations associated with the phrase and choose, instead, a descriptor more unambiguously linked to the improvement-oriented function of the activity. I see no particular phrase that hits the mark better than others, but I urge district administrators to select a descriptor such as "Teacher Growth Program," "Skill Enhancement System," "Professional Development Program," or "Personnel Improvement Activity." By using such descriptors, a positive response from teachers is far more likely.

Focusing on Effects, Not Process

Along with a name change, there must be a significant effort to separate improvement-focused teacher evaluation activities from the activities of summative evaluators.

The bulk of America's formatively oriented teacher evaluation systems are preoccupied with teachers' classroom behaviors. Typically, teachers are observed as they conduct their classes, then formatively evaluated on the basis of whether their behaviors were consonant with research-supported instructional principles. Such formative evaluation systems are conceptually flawed because they presume that research-derived principles, if adhered to by a specific teacher, will invariably lead to successful results with pupils.

Such is not the case. A specific teacher can violate many research-derived maxims, yet get fine results with children. Conversely, a teacher might adhere to a litany of research-derived guidelines, but produce pitiful progress in pupils. The conceptual flaw flows from the presumption that research-based conclusions such as "pupils tend to learn more if actively involved" automatically translate into, "Teacher X should be judged deficient if pupils are not actively involved." What *tends* to be true for large groups of teachers and pupils, however, may not be true in the case of a particular teacher. Teacher evaluation is a profoundly particular undertaking. When we evaluate Mary Smith's classroom performance, we must focus on Mary Smith—a *particular* teacher with a *particular* set of pupils in pursuit of *particular* goals and using *particular* educational materials in a *particular* classroom.

Process-focused teacher evaluation systems based on research-supported instructional mandates are empirically unsupportable because research-derived relationships between teacher behaviors and pupil progress are far from perfect. Such relationships, although perhaps "statistically" significant, are only suggestive, not definitive. Such tendency-type research results don't permit us to say whether a specific teacher who does/doesn't use such principles will achieve good results with learners.

Thus, even though attention to teachers' classroom behaviors can provide helpful hypotheses to formative teacher evaluators, the ultimate thrust of such evaluation must be rooted in what happens to pupils. Defensible formative teacher evaluation must be based on the growth that teachers bring about in students. Therefore, the formative evaluator must also be attentive to what learners become, not merely what teachers do. Classroom process, because of the complexities of classroom interactions, must be judged by the effects that teacher behaviors produce in children, not by the teacher behaviors themselves.

In practical terms, this means that the formative teacher evaluator must secure evidence of the extent to which pupils are prospering under a teacher's direction, then help the teacher determine the effectiveness of classroom practices according to their effects on learners.

Employ Pretest-Postest Evidence

One of the most straightforward ways to supply the teacher with an index of instructional impact is to contrast the performance of pupils following instruction with their performance prior to instruction. Yes, I am suggesting a simple pretest-posttest scheme for determining whether a teacher's instructional activities have any benefit for pupils. Research specialists, of course, point to a number of technical problems with gain scores. But for helping teachers discern whether their instructional tactics are working, pretest to posttest gains are quite serviceable.

We have to devise easy, nonintrusive ways of gathering evidence of pupil growth so that such evidence can be used as a major determinant of the teacher's instructional success. A number of simplification techniques can make such data-gathering easier. For example, to gauge a teacher's instructional impact, it is not necessary to test every student with the same test. Different pupils can be given only a few test items, but those items need not be the same for different pupils. By summarizing pupil results on the complete set of items, the teacher and formative evaluator can appropriately identify the effects of the teacher's instruction. Such an item-sampling scheme can help avoid the undesirable effects of pretesting where the pretest inappropriately sensitizes pupils to certain aspects of the instruction that will follow.

There are other schemes that skilled formative evaluators can use to make the formative data-gathering less intrusive and as easy and as efficient as possible. Ideally, the thrust of such data-gathering should be focused on a modest number of significant student outcomes. Formative evaluators should not overwhelm the teacher with tons of data. The teacher and formative evaluator can collaboratively decide what sorts of pupil pretest-postest evidence would be most helpful for establishing whether various types of classroom instructional practices are working.

A Sticky Wicket: Summative Teacher Evaluation

At the district level, summative teacher evaluation usually focuses on one of two significant decisions: tenure or termination. In the context of teacher evaluation, granting tenure to a teacher is a particularly important decision for district officials because the summative evaluation of a non-tenured teacher is meaningfully different from the summative evaluation of a tenured teacher. If a non-tenured teacher is judged incompetent, only modest evidence is needed to discharge the teacher. If a tenured teacher is regarded as incompetent, a far more formidable case must be built to support the allegation.

The dismissal of tenured and non-tenured teachers, therefore, constitutes two substantially different enterprises. However, the evidence-gathering and decision-making *operations* associated with both tenure and termination are fundamentally the same. District officials who wish to apply my recommendations will, I hope, be able to see the parallels between summative teacher evaluation for dismissal decisions and summative teacher evaluation for tenure decisions.

An Inadequate Technical Base

The technical foundation for summative teacher evaluators is infinitely more fragile than most educators recognize. Distressingly, we do not currently possess data-gathering procedures capable of providing us with compelling evidence that a particular teacher is competent or incompetent. A few examples of the weaknesses of prominent data-gathering schemes illustrate the shaky technical base for many current teacher evaluation schemes.

Classroom Observations. Classroom observations, for example, are prominently featured in many summative teacher evaluation approaches. Yet, as noted earlier, it is impossible to conclude from a particular teacher's use or non-use of research-based instructional procedures whether the teacher is actually getting good results from pupils. Research-rooted instructional procedures *tend* to promote pupil progress, but there is no certainty that a particular teacher who fails to employ such procedures will not achieve fine results. Moreover, classroom observations typically lead to a distortion of what goes on in a teacher's class; the presence of an observer usually influences the teacher's performance so that it is not typical of what normally transpires in the classroom. Observations based on atypical teacher performance tell little about a teacher's true level of competence. Thus, classroom observations, though widely used and almost universally regarded as important, yield data of only limited value to a summative teacher evaluator. A teacher who is about to be dismissed on the basis of evidence derived chiefly from classroom observations can marshal a solid attack on the validity of evaluative appraisals drawn from such evidence.

Pupil Growth. Another highly touted source of evidence for summative teacher evaluation is pupil growth, typically as reflected on teacher-made or standardized achievement tests. American educators are becoming increasingly aware of the profound insensitivity to instruction inherent in standardized, norm-referenced achievement tests. Although what happens to students as a consequence of instruction is patently important, summative teacher evaluators have been totally stumped by the problem of students' differential entry behaviors. If Teacher A is assigned a group of future Nobel Laureates while Teacher B is assigned a group of less able students, then the disparity between end-of-year test scores of the two classes, even on a properly constructed criterion-referenced test, signifies little about the two teachers' instructional skills.

We simply do not yet know how to deal with such differential entry behaviors. Some researchers contend that randomly assigning students to classes will help overcome this obstacle. Randomized assignment may satisfy the research-design requirements needs of researchers, but it is not apt to be accepted by parents or school districts. Nor can we use statistical mumbo-jumbo to equalize classes that are, in fact, composed of dramatically dissimilar youngsters. Statisticians who imply that such numerical magic is possible are simply promising more than they can deliver. And even pretest-to-posttest scores, although useful for formative evaluation, are not sufficiently defensible to use for summative evaluation. Thus, evidence of pupil growth, in spite of its importance, doesn't solve the summative evaluation puzzle.

The deficiencies associated with classroom-observation data and pupil-growth data are seen in other sorts of evidence-gathering conducted by summative teacher evaluators. Administrative ratings, peer evaluations, self-ratings, student ratings, and professional portfolios are laden with serious shortcomings. In short, no single source of data for summative teacher evaluation is sufficiently problem-free that it can form the cornerstone of a defensible summative teacher-evaluation program. Any district-level summative teacher-evaluation scheme that focuses only on one or two of these commonly used evaluation schemes is, without question, fundamentally flawed. Yet, it is apparent that if teachers are to be summatively evaluated, they must be evaluated on the basis of some sort of reasonable evidence. What, then, is the answer to this problem?

A Defensible Solution Strategy: Judgment-Based Teacher Evaluations

In many fields where the nature of professional practice is complex, personnel appraisal decisions are made chiefly on the basis of professional judgment. Qualified professionals review evidence relevant to an individual's competence, then render a judgmental appraisal. Although formal examinations, even paper and pencil ones, are sometimes used to secure evidence, in the final analysis personnel are appraised on the basis of professional judgment. We must do the same when we summatively evaluate teachers.

For over three decades I have been trying to discover a sensible scheme for evaluating teachers. The bulk of my effort was focused on a quest for quantitative indices of teacher competence, a quest that proved futile. I continually butted my head against the profound complexity of the teaching-learning process. Now I recognize that a problem this complex demands a solution that deals with such complexity. I therefore propose that district-level summative teacher appraisal programs be based on *judgment-based teacher evaluation* (J-BTE, pronounced "J-bite"). I also recommend that a J-BTE program rely on an amalgam of the same types of evidence that, if considered in isolation, constitute an indefensible index of a teacher's skill. At the heart of J-BTE is the ability of qualified professionals to consider various data sources, judge the soundness of such data, and reach conclusions about a teacher's competence in the context of the teacher's specific instructional setting. When compared with any alternative approach to summative teacher evaluation, J-BTE is far superior in reaching conceptually and legally defensible conclusions about a teacher's level of competence.

The Bases of J-BTE

JBTE is based on these two key tenets:

TENET 1: J-BTE relies on the *pooled professional judgment* of educators who have been *trained and certified* to make defensible judgments regarding teachers' *instructional competence.*

TENET 2: J-BTE requires that *multiple sources of evidence* be considered in the *context* of a teacher's instructional situation.

Pooled Professional Judgment. First, note that J-BTE involves *pooled professional judgment* by educators. Because the appraisal of a teacher is so complicated, it is clearly too risky to leave decisions as important as summative appraisal to one judge. At least three evaluators should pool their estimates so that, should one evaluator reach an inappropriate conclusion, two other evaluators will be able to provide more accurate judgments.

Training and Certification. It is clear that J-BTE evaluators must be educators who have been both *trained and certified* in J-BTE so that they are able to render defensible judgments. The training can be offered by the district or external trainers.

Experienced and able educators must be used as J-BTE evaluators so that the teachers will regard them as credible. Some would argue that it is wise to use teachers as J-BTE evaluators, because teachers will generally be more accepting of a judgmentally based teacher evaluation system in which teachers are evaluating other teachers. However, an effective argument can be made in favor of having skilled administrators as J-BTE evaluators.

Training and certification of evaluators are indispensable for J-BTE to prove successful. Judgment-based personnel appraisal efforts are sometimes discounted because they are thought to be arbitrary and unfounded. Indeed, arbitrariness is anathema to J-BTE. The conclusions reached by J-BTE evaluators must reflect carefully considered, data-based judgments. Because of the complexity of the phenomena involved, different J-BTE evaluators may at times reach different conclusions. Different people, of course, can reach different conclusions. Training and certification, however, can dramatically reduce the disparities in judgments reached by different teacher evaluators and teach the evaluators what to do when agreement is not reached initially.

If J-BTE is to be successful, its evaluators must be given a rigorous training program and must pass a demanding examination.

By far, the most difficult aspect of a teacher's performance to evaluate is the teacher's instructional competence. J-BTE focuses on providing an estimate of the teacher's instructional competence. It does not address the teacher's non-instructional responsibilities. If a teacher satisfactorily performs other job requirements, such as supervising extracurricular activities or holding district-mandated parent conferences, a negative J-BTE appraisal of the teacher's instructional competence could still be reached. Conversely, a teacher could fall down on all sorts of non-instructional responsibilities, yet secure a positive evaluation of instructional competence based on J-BTE.

Although there's more to a teacher's responsibilities than classroom instruction, because this is the most important of a teacher's responsibilities, J-BTE deals exclusively with an appraisal of instructional competence. How, then, should a district deal with noninstructional aspects of a teacher's performance?

Because the determination of a teacher's instructional competence is so difficult, I do not wish to saddle J-BTE evaluators with the additional task of determining whether a teacher satisfactorily discharges noninstructional responsibilities. Besides, school administrators seem to be doing pretty well in determining whether a teacher is performing acceptably with respect to noninstructional responsibilities.

Thus, I propose that a designated administrator, typically the principal, submit a separate evaluation of the teacher's performance regarding all those noninstructional responsibilities deemed important by the district. This evaluation of the teacher's effectiveness could be considered alongside the J-BTE evaluation of the teachers *instructional* competence. Figure 3.1 shows a scheme where district officials weigh two separate evaluations for a teacher.

Ideally, the school district's governing board would provide guidance about the relative importance of these two dimensions of a teacher's job

Figure 3.1
A Two-Dimensional Evaluation Scheme

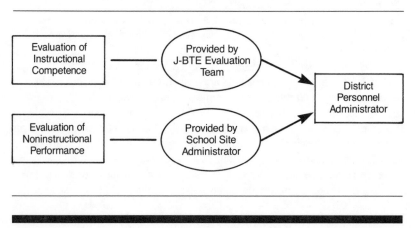

performance. There is no question that a teacher must be evaluated with regard to both instructional and non-instructional performance. It is difficult enough to deal with those two dimensions separately. Attempting to meld them is apt to cause confusion and be counter-productive.

Multiple Evidence Sources. Given the weaknesses in any single source of evidence regarding the teacher's instructional competence, J-BTE evaluators must rely on multiple sources of evidence. In essence, J-BTE evaluators should become familiar with the strengths and weaknesses of various types of evidence and then identify the quality of the particular types of evidence in the specific case. For instance, if a positive administrative rating of a teacher has been supplied by a principal who is notorious for never giving anything less than glowing ratings to teachers regardless of their competence, then the J-BTE evaluators should attach only modest meaningfulness to the principal's appraisal.

Having weighed the merits of all the types of available data, J-BTE evaluators must synthesize the sources so that the data patterns will be consistent and clear. Suppose, for example, that five different types of evidence are being used. (The number and types of evidence to be used in J-BTE can vary from district to district.) If the teacher appears weak on all five sources, it is likely that a negative judgment about instructional competence will be reached. Conversely, if all five sources of evidence are positive, then a positive J-BTE appraisal will surely be reached. If there are only minor inconsistencies in the set of evidence, then the J-BTE evaluator's task is fairly simple. If the evidence is discordant, however, with several very positive pieces of evidence countered by several very negative pieces of evidence, then J-BTE evaluators are apt to reach an inconclusive judgment about a teacher's skill.

In that case, the teacher should be reevaluated the following year, possibly with additional types of evidence. However, because in summative teacher evaluation we are often attempting to identify particularly inept teachers, a mixed set of credible J-BTE evidence resulting in a "hung jury" may suggest that the teacher being evaluated is not an across-the-board loser. It seems likely that the evidence regarding a truly incompetent teacher will typically be decisively negative.

Context Dependency. The final emphasis of J-BTE is the necessity to appraise a teacher's efforts in context. For years, officials of the National Education Association (NEA) have argued that teachers must not be uniformly evaluated as though context were unimportant. NEA's leaders argue that because instructional context is so pivotal, under no circumstances should a teacher be evaluated except by considering elements of the teacher's specific instructional situation. What may have, to some observers, been regarded as mere union rhetoric was, in fact, a commonsense conclusion that sometimes the same teacher, if placed in two very different settings, may function like two different people.

If Henry Hedley is given less than scintillating pupils, too few textbooks, and a poorly lighted classroom, he is apt to function less effectively then if he worked with super students and oodles of textbooks in a satisfactory classroom. Context makes an enormous difference in a teacher's instructional efforts. J-BTE evaluators must evaluate teachers in context of the particular instructional situation.

J-BTE Evidence Sources

J-BTE is a generic, judgmentally oriented approach to teacher evaluation that can be tailored to fit a school district's needs. It is not a highly structured, "one-size-fits-all" approach to teacher evaluation. Thus, a number of the elements to be described in the remainder of this chapter, such as the number of types of data sources to be used, can be altered at the district level.

We turn, now, to a consideration of several data sources that could be effectively used in a J-BTE approach to teacher appraisal. These data sources have been used in a J-BTE context during small-scale tryouts at UCLA in 1986-87 and, in a different context, by Kenneth Peterson while he was at the University of Utah. (Peterson has done some first-rate work in studying the utility of using different types of evidence for teacher evaluation.)

Five sources of data are particularly suitable for J-BTE. Each form of evidence, in itself, would be insufficient to judge a teacher's instructional skill. In concert, however, they provide a sufficient data base for a trained professional to reach a conclusion about a teacher's instructional competence.

Two criteria were used in scrutinizing possible data sources for J-BTE: (1) the potential power of the data source as a contributor to a professional judgment regarding a teacher's instructional skill and (2) the logistical ease of securing the data. The search was for a defensible approach to summative teacher evaluation that could be widely employed. Thus, not only did such a system's data need to yield plausible inferences about a teacher's skills, the system also had to be sufficiently practicable that it might be readily adopted. The five data sources are:

1. *Observations of classroom performance.*
2. *Administrative ratings of the teacher's instructional skill.* (Administrators serving as formative teacher evaluators would not supply administrative ratings.)
3. *Student evaluations of the teacher's instructional skill.*
4. *Reviews of teacher-prepared materials.*
5. *Evidence of student growth.*

Classroom Observations. Classroom observation data for J-BTE are based on at least three observations, one announced and two unannounced, made by different J-BTE evaluators. Thus, at minimum, a teacher would be observed on three different occasions by a different observer. These three individuals might also constitute a three-person J-BTE evaluation team. Each team member must observe the teacher on at least one occasion. Currently, J-BTE observers use a seven-category judgment form based on research-derived principles of effective teaching. Because the principles on which much of the seven-category judgment form is predicated are those used in direct instruction of well-organized content fields, J-BTE evaluators must recognize and make allowances for instructional situations where the teacher is pursuing goals not consonant with a direct-instruction strategy. The observation form's seven separate dimensions (five dealing with the lesson and two dealing with classroom management) are provided to assist the J-BTE evaluator in reaching an overall judgment of the teacher's instructional skill. That overall judgment is made by designating one of five evaluative choices: (exceptionally strong, strong, satisfactory, weak, or exceptionally weak).

Administrative Ratings. Administrative ratings are secured, typically from the teacher's principal, by asking an administrator for an overall judgment of the teacher's instructional skill based on formal or informal classroom observations made by that administrator. This administrative rating is totally separate and independent of the observations made by the three J-BTE evaluators. A school-site administrator can provide important insights about the teacher's instructional skill. Currently, an administrator checklist is employed for securing administrative ratings. As with a classroom observation form, the checklist is provided chiefly to help the administrator reach an overall judgment about the teacher's instructional skill. The administrative rating for J-BTE culminates in an overall rating, on a five-point scale, of the teacher's instructional competence.

However, if an administrator is already functioning on a formative evaluation capacity with teachers, then that administrator should not supply data relevant to the teacher's summative evaluation. To keep formative and summative teacher evaluation separate, it may be necessary at times to exclude administrative ratings from J-BTE. If individuals other than the school administrator are handling the formative evaluation chores, then administrative ratings should be tossed into the J-BTE data pool. If an assistant principal or head teacher are formative evaluators, then the principal should supply a summative rating of the teacher's instructional competence.

Recalling that it may also be the principal who supplies an evaluation of the teacher's noninstructional competence, it may appear that the principal is providing too much input to the teacher's evaluation. Remember, however, for the J-BTE evaluation of the teacher's instructional competence, an administrator's rating is only one of several sorts of data considered.

Student Evaluations. Student evaluations of teachers' skills have historically been employed only at the university level. During the past few years, however, there has been an increasing use of teacher evaluations by elementary, junior high, and high school students. In the early stages of work on the J-BTE model, we experimented with two versions of a student rating form. One, a short version, focuses on the key question of "How good is your teacher at teaching you things?" A longer version of the form has approximately 20 statements to which students answer yes or no in an effort to arrive at the same conclusion. In designing the forms, there was an effort to attend to the possible confounding influence, noted by Michael Scriven several years ago, of the extent to which the students are positively disposed toward the subject matter and the teacher as a person. Questions regarding both of these points are asked of the student before posing a direct question regarding the teacher's instructional skill.

Teacher-Prepared Materials. Another potential data category for J-BTE consists of reviews of teacher-prepared materials relevant to the teacher's instructional activities. These materials might include instructional materials, reading lists, activity descriptions, tests, lesson plans, examples of written feedback to pupils, classroom rules, classroom-specific discipline procedures, and written communications sent to parents.

Such materials, submitted by the teacher on the basis of a carefully developed series of guidelines and suggestions, are then judged by the J-BTE evaluation team. In carrying out this review, J-BTE evaluators can consult teachers who are more familiar with the teacher's grade level or subject. Judgmental criteria, particularized according to the types of materials involved, along with guidelines for reaching an overall five-point judgment about the quality of the teacher-prepared materials, are used in this review. As was the case with the other J-BTE sources of evidence, a review of teacher-prepared materials can contribute to an estimate of the teacher's instructional competence.

Student Growth. Evidence of student growth is to be assembled by the teacher. At the beginning of the academic year, the teacher is given a set of detailed J-BTE guidelines regarding the gathering of such evidence. In current versions of J-BTE guidelines, a variety of evidence can be presented by the teacher. Generally speaking, a pretest-instruction-posttest model is advocated. An important feature associated with this source of data is the necessity for the teacher to secure external reviews regarding the *quality* of the instructional aspirations reflected in the teacher's assessment approaches. The teacher is also given an opportunity to note any extenuating circumstances that might affect the extent of students' growth.

These are not the only indicators of a teacher's instructional competence that could be employed in a J-BTE approach to teacher evaluation. Nor is it necessary to use all five of the data sources described here. Some district policymakers, for example, might decide that the evaluation yield from teacher-prepared materials is too limited to warrant their inclusion in the district's J-BTE system. This is one of several important decisions to be made by those responsible for the district's teacher evaluation program.

Key Steps in J-BTE Implementation

District officials should follow these six steps to implement J-BTE evaluation.

Step 1: *Determine particulars of J-BTE:* make such decisions as the number of evaluators per J-BTE team and the types of evidence to be used.

Step 2: *Train and certify J-BTE evaluators:* provide training and certification-testing for potential J-BTE evaluators.

Step 3: *Gather designated evidence:* work with the teachers being evaluated to secure the types of evidence selected.

Step 4: *Assign weights to evidence:* based on the credibility and quality of each type of data, assign significance ratings to each.

Step 5: *Review all evidence:* consider each designated source of evidence regarding the teacher's instructional competence.

Step 6: *Reach pooled judgment:* group the judgments of all J-BTE evaluators to reach a conclusion regarding the teacher's instructional competence.

As indicated earlier, the J-BTE approach to teacher evaluation can definitely be tailored in local districts to take advantage of special circumstances and personnel.

J-BTE in Action

A team of three trained and certified J-BTE evaluators will typically gather, or be provided with, the sources of data for a teacher. Each of the evaluators will have had a first-hand opportunity to view the teacher in action.

Before reviewing the data, the J-BTE team will consider the context in which the teacher is functioning (i.e., quality of pupils, classroom facilities, instructional materials, and so on). The team will, as a group, assign relative weights to the five data sources in that particular setting for that particular teacher. Then, having reviewed the data, members of the J-BTE team will, first independently and then collectively, use the data sources to reach a pooled professional judgment regarding the teacher's instructional skill.

The data are to be used in a manner akin to that employed in the multiple-evidence validation strategies used in the field of measurement. If most of the highly weighted data sources point to the teacher's being a strong teacher, then the team will reach a positive summative judgment. If most of the highly weighted data sources suggest that the teacher is truly weak, the opposite judgment will be reached. If the data sources contradict one another, a more equivocal judgment is apt to be made.

The evaluation team will have to judge which of the data sources should be given more weight. For example, if a school district uses a particularly good set of criterion-referenced achievement tests, then the evaluators might wish to assign more weight to student growth as measured by those tests.

The J-BTE evaluators will consider all relevant data and contextual variables, then reach the best professional judgment they can make. This considered, pooled, professional judgment is the heart of J-BTE.

To illustrate the kinds of judgmental challenges faced by a J-BTE evaluation team, consider the two sets of fictitious data summaries presented in Figures 3.2 and 3.3 for two hypothetical teachers, Mr. Jenkin and Ms. Hill. The summarized data for all five evidence categories are presented as well as the J-BTE team's weighting of each evidence category's significance (high, moderate, low). If possible, these evidence-weighting decisions (based on the credibility and cogency of each type of evidence) should be made collaboratively by the J-BTE evaluation team before considering the evidence itself. For example, if five data sources are being used, each might be weighted equally. If, as a consequence of reviewing the actual data, four of the data sources are highly positive while one is highly negative, the J-BTE team will be apt to discount the one inconsistent data source.

In Figure 3.2 we see that, in this instance, the J-BTE team has weighted two data sources as most significant: classroom observations and pupil growth. Pupil evaluations, perhaps because of the 3rd grade children's age, are rated as being only moderately significant. The administrator's rating is also rated as only moderately significant. Perhaps the J-BTE team had learned that the administrator's ratings are notoriously haphazard. Finally, teacher-prepared materials were regarded by the J-BTE team in this situation to be of low significance. Perhaps the teacher failed to submit sufficient materials

Figure 3.2
A Fictitious J-BTE Data Summary

Teacher: Bill Jenkin		Grade: Third
Evidence Category	Judged Significance	Instructional Competence Indicated
Classroom Observations	High	Exceptionally Strong
Administrative Ratings	Moderate	Satisfactory
Student Evaluations	Moderate	Satisfactory
Teacher-Prepared Materials	Low	Weak
Student Growth	High	Strong

so that the J-BTE team was unable to reach reasonable conclusions about the teacher's material-producing quality.

Based on these team-determined judgments about the credibility and cogency of each data source, coupled with the summary indicators of instructional competence for each, it seems likely that the J-BTE team would reach a relatively positive appraisal of Bill Jenkin's instructional competence.

Let's try one more illustrative case, that is, the fictitious data summarized for Maria Hill in Figure 3.3. Because Maria's school district uses an excellent system of criterion-referenced achievement tests each semester, the J-BTE team ascribed high significance to the pupil growth category. Also, because the students in Hill's high school have had several years experience in supplying anonymous evaluations of teachers' skill, the J-BTE team viewed pupil evaluations as highly significant.

Figure 3.3
A Fictitious J-BTE Data Summary

Teacher: Maria Hill		Subject(s): English & Speech
Evidence Category	Judged Significance	Instructional Competence Indicated
Classroom Observations	Moderate	Weak
Administrative Ratings	Moderate	Strong
Student Evaluations	High	Weak
Teacher-Prepared Materials	Moderate	Satisfactory
Student Growth	High	Exceptionally Weak

Turning to the indications of instructional competence, we see that on the two categories of evidence judged to be most significant, Maria fared badly. Only the administrator's rating gives Maria a really positive mark. Although Maria's case is not an easy one, it seems probable that the J-BTE team would reach a negative summative judgment regarding her instructional competence.

Hopefully, these two illustrations make more clear how devilishly difficult it is to make determinations of a teacher's instructional skill when there are multiple evidence sources and, furthermore, when these sources of evidence are weighted differently. J-BTE is not simple because summative teacher evaluation is not simple. Complex problems demand sophisticated solutions. Qualified J-BTE evaluators can render the requisite sophisticated judgments that are needed.

Training and Certification

Clearly, the key to making J-BTE work satisfactorily for summative teacher evaluation is to have competent J-BTE evaluators operate the program. These evaluators must be systematically trained, then tested to verify that they are, indeed, competent. During a two- to three-week training session, J-BTE evaluators learn how to (1) gather the types of data that district officials decide to incorporate in the local J-BTE program, including in-class observations of teachers; (2) determine, in context, the significance of the resultant data; (3) aggregate and analyze all data; (4) reach defensible pooled judgments regarding a teacher's instructional competence; (5) document the case; and (6) adhere to due-process stipulations in the district's personnel contract.

The training program for J-BTE evaluators must be intensive and efficient. These individuals must learn about validity, reliability, evidence-weighting, and so on. The training program should culminate in a series of simulated evaluations in which trainees must deal with diverse data arrays for teachers, then reach conclusions regarding each teacher's instructional competence. Trainees should initially carry out these simulated J-BTE evaluations with substantial assistance from trainers, then gradually move toward independent judgment-rendering. Practice exercises for the final stages of a J-BTE training program have been prepared and can be made available to district officials interested in conducting their own J-BTE training sessions.

At the close of the training program, it is requisite to verify that the J-BTE evaluators are able to function with consistency and accuracy. Thus, a half-day certification examination must be given to all prospective J-BTE evaluators. Included in this certification examination are (1) videotaped classroom sessions that permit examinees to display their ability to make consistent and accurate observations, (2) simulated descriptions of teaching situations and displays of fictitious data that must be interpreted by examinees individually, and (3) simulated data that must be considered by three-person examinee teams, one member of which is an examinee. In short, the examinee must display skill in all aspects of the J-BTE process. Teachers who are to be evaluated by J-BTE evaluators must have confidence in the credibility of J-BTE personnel.

J-BTE as a Defensible Option

J-BTE is, of course, an evaluative scheme that rests squarely on the judgment of human beings. Will human beings commit errors when they make judgments? Of course! Should those errors dissuade district officials from adopting a judgment-based approach to teacher evaluation? Of course not!

Our nation's judicial system is predicated on the use of human judgment rendered by juries and judges. It is anticipated that, occasionally, juries or judges will err. There are, because of errors in courtrooms and juryrooms, some innocent persons serving prison sentences and some guilty persons walking the streets. Yet, over the years, our society has failed to come up with a better alternative. In dealing with the complexity of human conduct in the courtroom, we rely on human judgment because it's the best tool at our disposal.

Teacher evaluation is no different. Judgment-based teacher appraisal is not a flaw-free system of personnel evaluation. Mistakes will be made. Yet, J-BTE must be compared with the available alternatives. When such comparisons are honestly made, J-BTE wins—hands down.

I can think of a few more important tasks for district-level decision-makers than the identification and implementation of a defensible teacher evaluation program. Teachers who can be made more competent must be given the assistance to enhance their skills. Teachers who are incompetent, and cannot be improved, must be removed from our schools. The responsibility of American educators is to children, not teachers. We can discharge that responsibility by adopting defensible teacher evaluation programs.

References

McCarthey, S., and K. Peterson. "Peer Review of Materials in Public School Teacher Evaluation." *Journal of Personnel in Education.* (in press)

Millman, J. "Introduction." In *Handbook of Teacher Evaluation.* Beverly Hills, CA: Sage Publications, 1981.

Peterson, K. "Methodological Problems in Teacher Evaluation." *Journal of Research and Development in Education.* 17(4) (1984): 62-70.

Peterson, K, D. Stevens, and A. Driscoll. "Primary Grade Student Reports for Teacher Evaluation." *Journal of Personnel Evaluation in Education.* (in press)

Popham, W. J. "Teacher Evaluations: Mission Impossible." *Principal,* 65(4) (1986): 56-58.

Rosenshine, B. "Synthesis of Research on Explicit Teaching." *Educational Leadership* (1986): 60-69.

Scriven, M. "Summative Teacher Evaluation." In *Handbook of Teacher Evaluation,* edited by J. Millman. Beverly Hills, CA: Sage Publications, 1981.

Stiggins, R. "Teacher Evaluation: Accountability and Growth Systems—Different Purposes." *NASSP Bulletin,* (1986): 51-58.

JANET D. BRAND

From the Practitioner's Point of View...

At last someone has the courage to admit that teacher evaluation is judgmental! No matter how objective the criteria, from checklists to narrative summaries, any time one human being critiques the performance of another, the process involves judgment.

Popham's judgment-based approach combines the realities of the profession with the ideals of trust and integrity. However, there are three possible inhibitors to its success: (1) teachers may hesitate to trust that the formative and summative data will never meet, (2) they may also be reluctant to accept a differential weighting of summative evidence, and (3) principals may find it difficult to relinquish territorial dispositions because of their historical responsibility for staff selection and termination in "their buildings."

The success or failure of any new idea often depends on the implementation process. Popham readily admits that effective implementation of J-BTE requires a commitment of time, effort, and funding. If enough effort, enough funding, and, perhaps most important, enough time is invested by an organization willing to take such a humanistic approach to its evaluation process, the inhibitors can be overcome. The inevitable return will be achievement of the ultimate goal of all evaluation—improved performance.

Janet D. Brand, currently Elementary School Supervisor for the Seaford (Delaware) School District, has served as an elementary teacher, assistant principal for instruction, and an elementary school principal.

4 Teacher Performance Evaluation: A Total Systems Approach

RICHARD P. MANATT

I read Superintendent Jergens' rather unusual request for a proposal just before going to my Monday night class, which, appropriately enough, provides the 30 hours of state-mandated training for teacher evaluators in Iowa. The cause of the superintendent's request wasn't unusual—a dismissal attempt that failed. However, the request for a 30- to 40-page description of a practical approach to teacher evaluation was unusual. All too often, superintendents and headmasters just want an "instrument that's tough enough to fire teachers." Jergens quoted his board president, Maria Johnson, who wanted "consultants who know their stuff—a defensible teacher evaluation system—designed from the ground up!" He continued, "She wants it in two months, practical, cost-effective, consistent with what is known about teacher evaluation, and designed not only to remove incompetent teachers but also to improve the effectiveness of all of the district teachers."

The next morning I called Harry Jergens to learn more about his school organization so that a proper response could be written. The conversation also gave me an opportunity to explain how Shirley Stow and I operate the School Improvement Model (SIM) at the College of Education at Iowa State University.

Richard Manatt is Director, School Improvement Model Project, College of Educational Administration, Iowa State University.

The SIM research team helps public and independent schools improve student achievement by an organizational renewal process. Approximately a dozen team members (professors of education and research associates) join a "stakeholders' committee" appointed by the local board of education to measure, analyze, and improve the performance of all educational employees in an organization. The team strives for the "information organization" so essential to success in the decades ahead.

All teaching, writing, research, and extension activities center on the productivity of educators and schools. Because Jergens was mindful of cost and haste, I offer four general options.

Options

1. We could provide Jergens with a microcomputer-based evaluation system, licensed by the Iowa State University Research Foundation, called CATE/S (Computer Assisted Teacher Evaluation/Supervisor). This system serves individual schools or districts with more than 10,000 teachers (Manatt et al. 1986). CATE/S is intended for any school organization that wants a powerful, research-based, and comprehensive performance evaluation system for teachers without going through the lengthy process of developing and validating criteria, procedures, and improvement strategies. Currently, software is available for a number of microcomputers. The CATE/S diagnostic/prescriptive capabilities can also be adapted to any existing summative evaluation criteria, but in Jergens' case new criteria would be needed. A document reader is used for CATE/S when more than 30 or 40 teachers are evaluated (Manatt in progress).

2. Each school improvement model or performance appraisal system we have developed is copyrighted by a district or independent school. Jergens might wish to contact some of the districts we have worked with and ask to modify one of these programs.

3. A third option would be to participate in the development of a performance evaluation system for another group. Under this arrangement, one school organization understudies SIM consultants as they plan with a stakeholders' group in another district. Selected personnel from the visiting district would be afforded the professional courtesy of joining all of the planning and training sessions as well as receiving copies of all of the materials the SIM consultants use.

4. For Jergens' district, the fourth option is the most feasible: a three-year developmental process. Under this option, a consulting team from the SIM office would work with the district via a stakeholders' committee, which I have chosen to describe in detail.

How to Develop a Total-Systems Approach to Teacher Evaluation

The SIM approach to performance evaluation systems development is research-based and has repeatedly shown that teacher morale, educational climate, and student achievement improve (Manatt et al. 1976, Stow and Sweeney 1981, Manatt and Stow 1986, Manatt in progress).

Ever since our first modest effort to study teacher performance evaluation criteria 20 years ago, we have maintained a consistent set of principles that guide our work with a client district. First, SIM is a process, not a product. Each model is unique because it is planned for and operated and controlled by the teachers and administrators of that school organization. Therefore, the components vary but the philosophy does not.

The stakeholders' committee is appointed by the superintendent. The initial charge to the group makes clear that the task is important and that each member was appointed for special knowledge or skills. Stakeholders represent teachers, administrators, parents, students, and board members. No more than half of the stakeholders are teachers, who are typically selected by the leaders of their association or union. Stakeholders are informed at the outset that they are an ad hoc group serving at the pleasure of the board of education and that their assignment is to "decide to recommend"; the board must make the final policy decisions. Stakeholders committees vary from 15 to 25 members depending on the size of the school organization.

At first glance it might appear that the preponderance of teacher members would result in a watered-down performance appraisal system. This never happens for several reasons. Most important, teachers have higher standards than other stakeholders—a fact that may surprise some who haven't listened to teachers as individuals express their desires for professional respect and accomplishment. Second, teachers and administrators quickly become caught up in the challenge of creating an administrator performance evaluation system and a teacher performance evaluation system simultaneously. The opportunity to work toward a mutual-benefit appraisal system boosts expectations on all sides. Furthermore, teachers and administrators generally behave in a very professional manner when their clients (parents and students) are present.

Stakeholders are expected to serve for at least three years. In Year One, committee members plan a performance evaluation system for all professional positions. During the second year, and after approval by the board of education (and the collective bargaining process where required by law), each principal and a couple of teachers in each building test the proposed system. After careful analysis of the test, the system is refined and resubmitted to the collective bargaining process if required. Once approved, this new system is taught to all educational personnel. The total-systems approach to performance evaluation is used during the third year, and specific inservice activities are added for appropriate personnel. (Again, approval from the collective bargaining process may be required.)

Good organizations don't just measure your competence, they teach you to be more competent. Building on contemporary research bases of school effectiveness and classroom effectiveness, SIM activities include:

1. Evaluating and improving the performance of all administrators (including the superintendent and members of the board of education).

2. Evaluating and improving the performance of teachers.

3. Designing and implementing a staff development and training component to operate the new monitoring system successfully and to change administrative and teaching behaviors to maximize learning for students.

The stakeholders' committee will probably require 8 to 10 days of deliberation, spread over a school year, to create a total appraisal system.

School culture, the tradition of cooperation between teachers and administrators, and the labor climate in the district will all affect planning. Therefore, the stakeholder committee will want to participate in the following activities—which are options, not mandated steps:

1. Long-range strategic planning.

2. Evaluating the performance of all board members, administrators, and teachers.

3. School improvement planning by school site personnel.

4. Curriculum mapping or planning.

5. Curriculum articulation, alignment, and monitoring.

6. Feedback solicitation from students and parents.

7. Development of a contemporary supervisory model (collaborative developmental, peer coaching).

8. Offering staff development options depending on needs or interests (TESA, GESA, Essential Elements of Effective Instruction, Cooperative Learning).

9. Developing a record- and report-making system.

10. Improving the school climate.

Figure 4.1 graphically depicts the school improvement model.

Notice that up to this point nothing has been said about the "need to remove bad teachers." Instead, the system is a due-process supervision approach that, when evidence warrants, may be used to create a subsystem of the total evaluation program to supervise the marginal teacher. Anticipate, however, that the specter of a failed attempt to dismiss an employee will cast a long shadow and influence the thinking and deliberations of the stakeholders.

Figure 4.1
The School Improvement Model

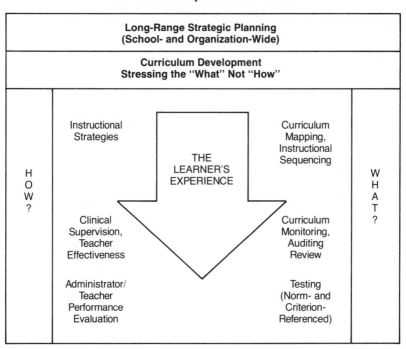

How to Develop the Stakeholders' Activities

The stakeholders' committee is led by two cochairs: a consultant from the SIM office and an administrator from the school district. The district cochair is called the "field coordinator" and is often an assistant superintendent in a larger district or a principal in a smaller district. Using a structured set of experiences (School Improvement Model Office 1987) developed by the SIM team, the stakeholders follow the plan detailed in Figure 4.2. The overall plan and the kit materials follow the recommendations of the Joint Committee on the Standards for Educational Evaluation (1986).

The stakeholders' first, and most difficult, task is to determine the purposes of an articulated performance appraisal system. Our experience has shown that, generally speaking, stakeholders identify six functions of a performance appraisal system.

1. To improve teaching and administration (identify ways to change teaching systems, environments, behaviors, change-management systems, and climate behaviors).

2. To supply information that will lead to modification of assignments, such as placement in other positions, promotions, or terminations.

3. To protect students from incompetent teachers and teachers from unprofessional administrators.

4. To reward superior performance.

5. To validate the school organization's teacher/administrator selection process.

6. To provide a basis for teachers' and administrators' planning and professional development.

In states with career ladders and those with mandated pay for perfor-

Figure 4.2
Plan for Developing an Articulated
Teacher and Administrator Performance Evaluation System

Phase	Activity	Questions/Topics
I.	Select committees* Survey and interview to determine administrative and instructional "situation."	Steering Committee (Subcommittee Chairpersons) 1. Philosophy and objectives 2. Performance areas and criteria 3. Operational procedures 4. Forms and records 5. Test and field test
II.	Subcommittees set specifications for teacher and administrator performance evaluation.	
	1. Steering Committee	a. Create/manage timeline b. Inform/consult superintendent and board c. Determine consultant usage d. Determine performance vs. input-output evaluation e. Inform/consult staff
	2. Philosophy and Objectives	a. Why evaluate administrators? Teachers? b. Shall we use multiple evaluators? c. What constitutes good administration in this district? Effective teaching?

*All committee activities must be guided by the constraints of appropriate state statutes.

Phase	Activity	Questions/Topics
	3. Performance Areas and Criteria	Aids administration in determining: a. What performance areas count? b. What about leadership vs. management? c. What specific criteria within these areas? d. Benchmark of teaching effectiveness
	4. Operational Procedures	a. If we use multiple evaluators, how do we do it? b. What should be the cycle? c. What should constitute an appraisal conference? d. How should feedback and help be provided?
	5. Forms and Records	a. Analysis of system b. How do we streamline paperwork? c. Do we need separate documents for formative and summative data? d. Should there be a program evaluation form?
	6. Test and Field Test	a. What constitutes an appropriate test of the new system? b. What are our criteria of validity, reliability, discrimination power? c. When should we begin the field test? d. How high shall our standards be? e. What orientation and training is needed for the evaluators?
III.	Set philosophies; determine criteria to be used.	Inform all subcommittees of guidelines. Strive for agreement: teachers, administrators, board, students, community. Orient evaluators and evaluatees?
	Describe cycle to be used. Draft forms and records.	Conferences, observations, coaching. How to document what happens—specify performance changes needed, give credit for success!
	Plant cut-and-try experiment.	Who? What? When? Where? Why? For how many dollars?
	Field test, review, rewrite.	What worked? What did not? What more do we need?
	Establish and improve.	Operate staff interventions: skills training for evaluators, improve teacher/administrator performance, check against previous evaluation; orient, orient, and reorient!

mance (approximately 30 at this writing), rewarding superior performance requires a great deal of attention. In other states, "reward" is simply a good evaluation and positive reinforcement from the supervisor.

Once determined, the evaluation functions enable the stakeholders to state a philosophy of evaluation. Customarily, the stakeholders' committee also writes or updates the district's philosophy of education and creates a philosophy of administration.

The Essentials of a Performance Evaluation

Irrespective of the job being evaluated, four key questions must be asked for every performance evaluation.

1. What are our criteria?
2. How high are our standards?
3. How should we monitor and report progress?
4. How shall we help the evaluatee improve after we have identified a profile of strengths and weaknesses?

A SIM research team has spent 20 years attempting to answer each of these questions.

What Are Your Criteria?

Starting in the late 1960s, SIM researchers created a generic job description for classroom teachers (Manatt et al. 1976) and identified hundreds of possible performance criteria. We sought criteria that were valid, reliable, and discriminating. Because validity means truthfulness, we used research on teaching to validate the criteria (Manatt and Stow 1984). Reliability means consistency, and we sought criteria that afforded both interrater and individual reliability (Hidlebaugh 1973, Peterson in press). Discrimination power means that the criteria can separate high teacher performance from average and subpar performance. Figure 4.3 lists a ranking of such criteria.

The criteria are provided with a response mode in the form of a behaviorally anchored rating scale (BARS). At various times and with various school organizations, the SIM researchers have used (for both formative and summative instruments) a variety of techniques including the BARS graphic response. The BARS approach is most effective when reliability, discrimination power, and the ability to compare one teacher to another are required. The BARS response also allowed for a statement of standard performance (see Figure 4.4).

All of the validated criteria are made available to the stakeholders on a large matrix (and in a research-based manual) for their selection.

Figure 4.3
Order of Discriminating Teacher Performance Criteria

1. Maintains an effective relationship with students' families.
2. Provides instruction appropriate for capabilities, rates of learning styles of students.
3. Prepares appropriate evaluation activities.
4. Communicates effectively with students.
5. Monitors seatwork closely.
6. Demonstrates sensitivity in relating to students.
7. Promotes positive self-concept in students.
8. Promotes students' self-discipline and responsibility.
9. Uses a variety of teaching techniques.
10. Spends time at the beginning of the learning demonstrating processes to the student (cueing).
11. Uses controlled (guided) practice before assigning homework (independent practice).
12. Organizes students for effective instruction.
13. Provides students with specific evaluative feedback.
14. Selects and uses appropriate lesson content, learning activities, and materials.
15. Demonstrates ability to monitor student behavior.
16. Writes effective lesson plans.
17. Demonstrates a willingness to keep curriculum and instructional practices current.
18. Has high expectations.
19. Organizes resources and materials for effective instruction.
20. Models and gives concrete examples.

This list is a composite of discriminating criteria used by one or more of the original SIM school organizations.

Figure 4.4
Graphic Response Model Teacher Performance Criterion

Performance Area I: Productive Teaching Techniques

Criterion: The teacher demonstrates ability to select appropriate learning content.

Levels of Performance: STANDARD

Not observed	Learning content not related to approved curriculum guide(s).	Learning content is marginally related to the approved curriculum.	Learning content is related to the approved curriculum guide(s).	In addition to meeting the standard, the teacher shows initiative and leadership in review and development of curriculum.

This partial list is an illustration only.

How High Are Your Standards?

The issue of performance standards is of paramount importance. None of the 50 states has an adequate definition of an incompetent teacher, but all of them have case law that supports the prerogative of management to set work standards. Thus, a superintendent and school board have the opportunity to embed work standards in the position description and in the performance criteria used to form a summative evaluation instrument. Later, if a teacher's performance is poor, dismissal can be based on "failure to meet work standards."

Performance standards are more than simply a solution to the lack of a legal definition of teaching incompetence, however. Once they are in place, the district can hire and coach employees to meet those work standards and provide training to the standards.

Performance standards are not static. They will go up over time, especially with the addition of more training or technology. Examples of such change are the use of individualized educational plans in special education since the changes in federal law, and the need for mathematics and science instructors to be computer literate.

The use of performance standards in the development of the instruments used for the appraisal system is crucial if, subsequent to the implementation of the appraisal component, some teachers must be removed for cause. Procedural and substantive due process both depend, in large part, on proper notice, that is, "What is expected of me as an employee?"

A side issue in the matter of standards often arises in the stakeholders' discussion of performance criteria. Some members of the group (usually teachers) will say, "Of course we will only use classroom performance to evaluate teachers." When that rather narrow focus is used, the eventual confrontation with the school board will sound like this.

Board member: I see you only have criteria dealing with the teacher's performance in the classroom.

Chair of the stakeholders: That's right, Mr. Blank. We wanted to measure teaching in the classroom.

Board member: But, Ms. Chair, we have some teachers who are perfectly adequate when they're in the classroom; the problem is that they're lousy employees. They come to work late and they abuse sick leave. What about them, Ms. Chair?

The proper answer is that criteria are needed for employee rules as well as classroom performance. Consistent violation of employee rules leads to progressive discipline action, while subpar teaching may eventually result in the use of an intensive assistance plan. These are two quite different problems, but both must be included in the notice, explanation, assistance, and time of due process supervision. (An easy memory crutch for this list is "due process supervision is NEAT.")

How Shall We Monitor and Report Progress?

This question is the stumbling block for almost half of the performance appraisal systems we have studied. The most difficult questions regarding procedures arise because:

1. Most principals are ill-prepared to work as clinical supervisors.

2. School organizations attempt to make sweeping changes in their teacher evaluation procedures without changing how principals "keep score," getting control of the motivation matrix for principals via changes in a job description, and establishing performance criteria for principals. A school will never have valid, reliable, and legally discriminating performance appraisal for teachers until it has such an appraisal for principals. Some school organizations have had noticeable success by only improving principal performance evaluation; few have been successful by changing only the teacher performance evaluation system.

3. School organizations seldom face up to the fact that their principals monitor too many employees for effective supervision. In the private sector, a ratio of 1 supervisor for 10 to 15 employees is standard. Many principals supervise over 100 professionals as well as several dozen aides, custodians, and secretaries. Facing these odds, is it any surprise many principals lament that they don't have time to properly advise teachers? Unfortunately, some teachers and some teachers' organizations build upon these feelings of inadequacy to denigrate teacher evaluations and those who conduct them. A number of constructive steps will help.

Not all of the activities of formative and summative performance evaluation must be assigned to principals. All teachers do not need all performance appraisal steps in a given year. (Unless, of course, pay-for-performance is on an annual cycle). Most important, modern technology such as micro-based, artificial intelligence programs may be used to lighten, by half, the record keeping and decision-making time (Manatt in progress). In fairness, it should be noted that rating teachers for an end-of-the-year summative evaluation and actually helping them extend and refine their skills during formative evaluation require much different time commitments.

Figure 4.5 is a comparison of formative and summative evaluation of teachers and administrators. To have a payoff for all stakeholders, you use both formative and summative performance evaluation in a continuing cycle, using modern technology to provide valid, reliable, and legally discriminating teacher performance evaluation. Formative evaluation is ongoing, descriptive, nonjudgmental, and performed to help teachers teach better.

Summative evaluation, at the end of a formative cycle, is comparative

Figure 4.5
How Formative Evaluation Differs From
Summative Evaluation in Performance Appraisal
of the Education Professional

FORMATIVE		SUMMATIVE
To help teachers teach better (Ongoing, descriptive, developmental, nonjudgmental)		To help management make better decisions (Final, judgmental, comparative, adjudicative)
	PHILOSOPHY	
Each individual strives for excellence		Individuals achieve excellence only if supervised or evaluated by others
	THEORY	
Evaluation is done to improve performance of the individual; reward or punishment is internal (learning theory)		Evaluation is done to improve the school organization and/or society; reward or punishment should be done externally (testing theory)
	PRACTICE	
Evaluate the process of instruction, not the person, "coaching"		Evaluate the products of instruction as well as the process and the person, "comparing and sorting"
	FOCUS	
Bottom up, holistic, free agency, serve me, for *me*		Top down, analytic, serve all stakeholders, for mutual benefit
	APPRAISER	
A team approach, renewal		The first-line supervisor, accountability
	CONTINUUM	
Clinical supervision	Professional evaluation	Weed out (Bureaucratic evaluation)

and judgmental and, if the teacher is a subpar performer, may become adjudicative. Formative evaluation is performed to help managers make better decisions. (In this context, management extends right up to the state education officer, the legislature, and the governor.)

Lamentably, much of what has been done during the reform movement of the '80s has beefed up summative evaluation at the expense of formative evaluation. In training hundreds of administrators to evaluate for career ladders and merit pay, the SIM team has learned that the minute money is hooked to ratings, all attention is focused on the summative evaluation conference. Indeed, the whole environment changes for principals when differential compensation is introduced. I liken training principals to evaluate teachers for pay (after years of evaluating only for improvement of instruction) to training jockeys to drive the Indianapolis 500!

How much classroom observation is enough? That question is as vague as the query to Abe Lincoln, "How long should a man's leg be?" Supposedly he answered, "Long enough to reach the ground." The number of classroom visits depends on many variables: Is the teacher a novice or a master? Is the teacher tenured or probationary? Are you doing skills-refining or confidence-building, or helping the teacher make new skills a permanent part of the repertoire?

From a strictly due process supervision approach, the teacher's class should be visited more than once each semester. Some of these visits should be announced; some should be drop-by visits. Generally speaking, principals spend too little time with their aces and too much time with rookies and marginal teachers. That is not to say that rookies and marginal teachers don't need lots of attention, but it doesn't have to be from the principal. Figures 4.6 and 4.7 contain the steps in the performance evaluation process used by a recent SIM school-district client (Garvey School District 1987).

How Shall We Help the Teacher Improve After We Have Identified a Profile of Strengths and Weaknesses?

Aside from the feedback given in the postobservation conference, two other answers are obvious. The well-known RAND report (Wise et al. 1984), after a detailed study of all of the components of the teacher performance evaluation cycle, concluded that the written agreement between the appraiser and appraisee for the improved performance in the next cycle is the most potent part of teacher evaluation.

A written agreement between the appraiser and appraisee has been described as a "job improvement target" made between the principal and a teacher (Redfern 1980). Other, more recent terminology is "professional improvement commitment" (Stow in press) or "professional growth plan." The latter term has been generally adopted in career ladder states. The SIM research team has written, field-tested, and validated a series of these agreements for all of the more frequently used teacher performance evaluation criteria (Stow et al. 1987, Stow in press).

The second answer for improved performance has to be staff development, but staff development that is integrated with supervision and teacher performance evaluation. The idea of an integrated approach has been around

Figure 4.6
Steps in the Performance Evaluation Process

I. Formative Evaluation Process

Step 1   *Self-Evaluation Form:*
To be completed by evaluatee prior to the Planning Conference.

Step 2   *Planning/Goals-Setting Conference:*
A. Review evaluation procedures.
B. Review self-evaluation form and leave copy with evaluator.
C. Evaluatee and evaluator establish or review the professional growth plan(s) for the next cycle. The growth plan consists of the following:
   1. goal
   2. objective of expected outcomes
   3. plan of action and timeline
   4. progress check(s)
   5. appraisal method for final accomplishment

Step 3   *Preobservation Conference:*
Held prior to the first scheduled observation to discuss the completed observation data report. Preconference for the second formal observation is optional.

Step 4   *Observation:*
Classroom/worksite observation by evaluator using observation data report.
(Informal observations may be held at anytime.)

Step 5   *Postobservation Conference:*
To be held within five working days following all formal observations, or as soon as possible.

II. Summative Evaluation Conference

Step 6   A. Evaluatee must be notified 10 working days prior to conference so that supporting data may be submitted to evaluator.
B. Evaluatee has a minimum of five days to provide supporting data, if desired.
C. Evaluator completes summative evaluation report conference.
D. Evaluator and evaluatee meet and discuss summative evaluation report.
E. Evaluatee may respond, in writing, to summative evaluation report within seven working days.
F. Evaluatee and evaluator establish professional growth plan short- and long-range targets for next evaluation cycle.

Source: Garvey School District, Certified Evaluation System, Rosemead, Calif.: June 1987.

for a long time. Too often, staff development is a large-group experience with a professor from a nearby teachers' college giving all personnel the same workshop on a "hot topic." In any such audience, some of the teachers could present the topic as well as the professor, many of the teachers don't need the training, and only a few find the training helpful. What is needed is a way

Figure 4.7
The Teacher Performance Evaluation Cycle

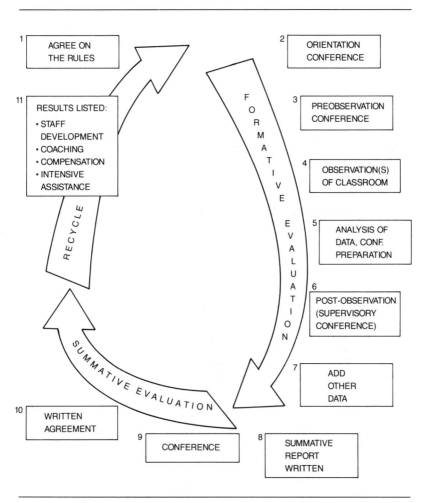

to use the performance appraisal data pertaining to each teacher to generate rosters of those teachers who need specific help. Computer Assisted Teacher Performance Evaluation/Supervision (CATE/S) can be used for this task and most of the other analyses in reportmaking for both "written agreements" and staff development needs reports. The idea for CATE/S came from a news release from the *New England Journal of Medicine* on an "artificial intelligence" microcomputer program called CADUCEUS. In diagnosing and prescribing, CADUCEUS routinely solved the monthly medical puzzles in the Journal as well as live practitioners. A similar program was written to serve principals, personnel officers, and staff development directors (Manatt in progress). The written agreement SIM recommends for use in teacher performance evaluation is shown in Figure 4.8.

When the work of a stakeholders' committee is finished, a handbook of teacher performance evaluation is created. Parallel booklets for administrators and educators with nonteaching assignments are also produced. The contents typically include philosophies of education, instruction, and evaluation; steps

Figure 4.8
Written Agreement for Improved Performance

AREA:	Productive Teaching Techniques
CRITERION: (1.1.10)*	Demonstrates effective planning skills.
PIC:	Prior to the beginning of the next semester the teacher will write long-range goals for the course being taught
PROCEDURES:	1. Review curriculum goals. 2. Identify content focus and learning outcomes. 3. Identify student needs. 4. Write long-range goals. 5. Submit goals to the evaluator.
TIMELINE:	Define the time in terms of weeks, months, or other segments for each step of the procedures.
MONITORING:	A progress check that could include formal or informal observations, a work sample, etc.
EVIDENCE:	Written long-range goals.
STANDARDS:	Please check one or more of the following: ☐ District policy ☐ Building procedures ☐ Research-based model ☐ Other (please specify)
APPRAISAL METHOD:	The evaluator will compare written long-range goals with the standard.
INDICATORS OF ACCOMPLISHMENT:	Fully Partially Not accomplished
RESEARCH EVIDENCE:	See Clinical Manual pp. 4-6.*

*From Manatt, R. P., and S. B. Stow. *The Clinical Manual for Teacher Performance Evaluation*. Ames: Iowa State University Research Foundation, 1984.

in the performance evaluation process; and formative and summative instruments. The instruments are for conference reports, classroom observations, summative evaluation reports, and professional growth plans. At some time in the planning process, the idea is, "Let's just use one form!" Another stakeholder will chime in, "Yes, and let's put everything on one side of the page!" It can be done, but why settle for a Swiss army knife when you can have the whole bag of tools? The most common teacher evaluation documents in a manual system are illustrated in Figures 4.9-4.11.

Field Testing and Training

The second year of a three-year project calls for rigorous training of all evaluators, a thorough orientation for all teachers, and a test of the procedures and instruments. This discussion deals chiefly with how training is provided.

Perhaps the most crucial element of performance appraisal is the development of mutual trust and credibility. Teachers' effectiveness could be determined without classroom observation—but teachers wouldn't believe it. Principals and other evaluators earn their credibility, in large part, by "walking in the teachers' moccasins" through classroom observation and modeling effective teaching behaviors in coaching. We have found that the quickest way to develop this credibility is to train teachers and administrators together. Indeed, in career ladder states where classroom teachers must serve as the "second appraiser," we have discovered teachers can be made reliable, accurate appraisers faster than some experienced principals, who seem to have a lot of unlearning to do! For either group, the skills include:

1. Identifying and analyzing effective teaching and effective performance behaviors.

2. Analyzing lesson design, teaching artifacts, and relevant student data.

3. Observing, recording, and reporting in the classroom.

4. Conducting effective evaluation conferences.

5. Developing a growth or improvement plan.

6. Developing an understanding of the purposes and legal aspects of performance evaluation (Iowa Department of Education 1987).

The "artifacts" of teaching include lesson plans, tests, reading lists, course outlines, samples of students' work, and handouts used in class. Teacher-made tests are especially useful when determining the curriculum alignment among content, instruction, and assessment.

SIM has produced a series of video-based learning albums, distributed by ASCO, which are suitable for training appraisers of teachers. Each tape series features several teachers, and their performances have been analyzed and evaluated by expert juries and a national sample of appraisers that con-

Figure 4.9
Formative Instrument (Teacher Evaluation)

Class Taught —————— Grade —————— Period —————— Teacher ——————

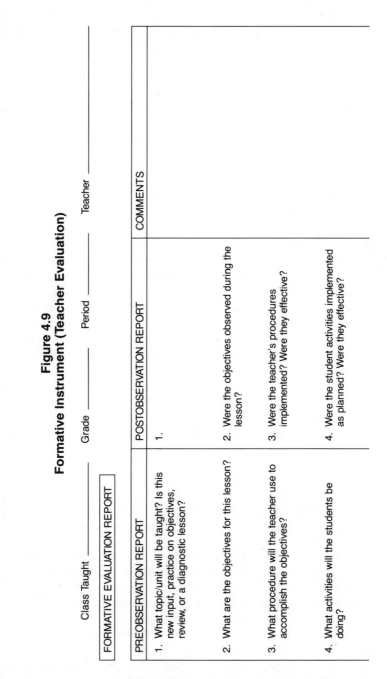

FORMATIVE EVALUATION REPORT

PREOBSERVATION REPORT	POSTOBSERVATION REPORT	COMMENTS
1. What topic/unit will be taught? Is this new input, practice on objectives, review, or a diagnostic lesson?	1.	
2. What are the objectives for this lesson?	2. Were the objectives observed during the lesson?	
3. What procedure will the teacher use to accomplish the objectives?	3. Were the teacher's procedures implemented? Were they effective?	
4. What activities will the students be doing?	4. Were the student activities implemented as planned? Were they effective?	

5. Which particular criterion/criteria do you want monitored?

Performance Area I
A. Demonstrates effective planning skills
B. Implements the lesson plan to ensure time on task.
C. Provides positive motivational experiences
D. Communicates effectively with students
E. Provides for effective student evaluation
F. Displays knowledge of curriculum and subject matter
G. Provides opportunities for individual differences
H. Demonstrates skills in classroom management
I. Sets high standards for student behavior

5. Indicate pertinent data gathered relevant to the criteria.

Figure 4.10
Summative Evaluation Report (Teachers)

PERFORMANCE AREA I: TEACHING TECHNIQUES

CRITERIA		LEVELS OF PERFORMANCE			
	Not Observed	Does Not Meet	Needs Improvement	Meets Standard	Exceeds
A. Demonstrates effective planning skills. COMMENTS:	N/O	Does not demonstrate effective planning skills.	Inconsistently demonstrates effective planning skills.	Demonstrates effective planning skills.	Qualifies as a model for effective planning skills.
B. Implements the lesson plan to ensure time on task. COMMENTS:	N/O	Does not implement the lesson plan effectively.	Inconsistently implements the lesson plan.	Effectively implements the lesson plan.	Qualifies as a model on how to effectively implement a lesson plan.

	N/O			
C. Provides positive motivational experiences.		Sets unrealistic expectations which dissuade students from performing according to their abilities.	Usually motivates students to perform assigned tasks but inconsistently requires students to perform according to their abilities.	Clearly expects and motivates students to perform assigned tasks according to their abilities.	Qualifies as a model for designing and implementing motivational experiences.

COMMENTS:

	N/O			
D. Communicates effectively with students.		Communications are frequently unclear; students often appear confused.	Communications are usually clear but student input is not encouraged.	Communications are clear; relevant dialogue is encouraged.	Qualifies as a model for effective communications.

COMMENTS:

Figure 4.11
Written Agreement for Improved Performance

Job Improvement Target Form
(for teachers other than counselors and librarians)

Name _____   Subject/Grade _____

Building _____   Date _____

One job improvement target form should be completed for each job target written.

PERFORMANCE AREA:	Criterion from Summative Evaluation
_____ Teaching Techniques	Report on which TARGET is based:
_____ Positive Interpersonal Relations	
_____ Professional Responsibilities	

I. GOAL (general intent)

II. SPECIFIC, MEASURABLE BEHAVIOR: (What will be done?)

III. PROCEDURES: (How will it be done?)   When to be
    Steps: accomplished

IV. PROGRESS CHECKS: (How is it going?)
EVALUATOR'S COMMENTS:

V. DOCUMENTATION/APPRAISAL METHOD FOR FINAL ACCOMPLISHMENT OF
    TARGET: (How will you know it was done?)
    Written evidence

    Appraisal method

    Standard(s)

EVALUATOR'S COMMENTS:	EVALUATEE'S COMMENTS:
The target was:	
_____ Not Accomplished	
_____ Partially Accomplished	
_____ Fully Accomplished	
Signature _____ Date	Signature _____ Date

stitute a norm group. Descriptions of each class and teaching artifacts are provided along with an instructor's manual that details the use of simulations for evaluator training. The greatest value of these materials is the opportunity to determine interrater reliability and to highlight possible biases.

Possible Rater Bias in Teacher Evaluation

Only so much can be accomplished by good instrumentation. Inevitably, instruments require compromises in length, descriptors, indicators, and high- vs. low-inference criteria. Low-inference criteria facilitate interrater reliability, but low-inference items (such as the number of times the teacher smiles per class period) trivialize teaching.

Bias, more properly called human error in rating performance, comes in five forms: (1) leniency/severity/central tendency, (2) halo effect, (3) rater characteristics, (4) rater position, and (5) personal bias. The usual remedy for bias is "more training"; however, some bias is so ingrained that only multiple appraisers and special "bias feedback" will help (Strahan 1980, Etaugh and Foresman 1983). Few researchers have studied the human factors that influence the quality of appraisal ratings (Ilgen 1983). Even fewer have dealt with bias in educational performance evaluation (Peterson in press).

Leniency/Severity/Central Tendency

The few studies of judging human performance acknowledge that performance evaluation is an activity based on a certain amount of subjectivity. Some evaluators refuse to differentiate between levels of performance of raters by clustering their scores in a narrow range, generally around the "mean." Such an error is called central tendency bias.

Severity error (deliberate low ratings) is much rarer. It has been prevalent in many military organizations in initial training situations (i.e., boot camp, basic training, and initial flight training). Interestingly, severity bias in U.S. military ratings promptly disappears once a person becomes an officer.

How ratings are to be used influences leniency. In the original School Improvement Model, the SIM team had school principals rate teachers they planned to conference with regarding improvement. Later, the school principals were asked to rate teachers for research purposes. The ratings that were to be shown teachers during a conference were substantially higher than those to be used for research. It appears, then, that there are two standards: one if the rating is used for research purposes and another (more lenient) if the results are to be used for administrative decisions, such as promotion or demotion.

Halo Bias. Halo effect results when evaluators let their ratings be unduly influenced by the overall impression of the person being rated (Landy and Farr 1980, Doyle 1983, Pulakos 1984). Perhaps the most common halo effect is the "nice guy" syndrome. Some employees are well-liked and get along with supervisors and peers alike. For this reason, the employee is rated high on all evaluation criteria. Teachers who follow the particular model of instruction that is favored by the school principal often cause a halo effect.

The halo effect can be reduced through at least three strategies: having multiple raters, having the evaluator rate all employees on a single criterion before moving on to the next criterion and not looking back on the ratings previously assigned to the teacher, and making the rating scale benchmarks more specific by using Behaviorally Anchored Rating Scales (BARS) where indicators and descriptors reduce subjectivity (Wexley and Yukl 1984).

Rater Characteristics. There is growing evidence that certain traits possessed by the person conducting an evaluation can influence the accuracy of the ratings. Personal competence as a supervisor, educational level, experience, and gender can all influence ratings.

Rater Position. Those who have worked for any length of time in a large-scale bureaucracy have observed that the higher up the boss is, the less he or she is satisfied with the work of the rank and file. Superintendents, for example, often jawbone principals for their lenient ratings of teachers. Moreover, studies show that peers rate more leniently than supervisors (Doyle 1983).

Personal Bias. Perhaps the most dangerous bias of all, personal bias, allows factors such as physical attractiveness, race, ethnic background, and social standing in the community to distort performance appraisals. This phenomenon has been described as the like me/not like me biases (Henderson 1984).

Bias and Evaluation Training

The SIM research team has long speculated that, given enough training and multiple appraisers, most biases will wash out. When designing and implementing a teacher performance evaluation system for a large southern school district with a sizable minority teaching force and a career-ladder compensation plan, all five types of rater bias were examined. All appraisers had received at least 10 days of specialized appraiser training and were fully aware of the rating's impact on teachers' movements on the career ladder and eventual differences in compensation. The results revealed: (1) Females rated male and female teachers significantly lower than did male evaluators. (2) Hispanic evaluators had the lowest average ratings; blacks rated teachers slightly higher than the average but still significantly lower than the average ratings of white principals. (3) Ratings varied by the amount of formal education. Evaluators with more than a master's degree rated teachers significantly higher on the average. (4) Experience made a difference. Evaluators in the 11- to 15-year cohort were much tougher than their colleagues with more or less experience. (5) Interactions of gender and race were analyzed but found to be not significant. (6) Distance in the organization as measured by first or second appraiser (the second being from a different campus) had no effect on ratings. (7) The ratings were checked for consistency across semesters. The first semester appraisal scores appeared to be very accurate predictors of the second semester ratings.

The SIM research suggests that these biases must be dealt with in most teacher evaluation systems. Some district officials may decline to train evaluators in bias saying, "But we have few minority administrators or teachers." However, the most pronounced differences were for gender and for amount of education, and most districts now have (or are struggling to have) some female administrators and some administrators with six-year and doctoral degrees. Extensive training for the appraisal role, multiple appraisers, and prior awareness of the likelihood of bias (using video simulations rather than real teachers) all will help reduce rater bias.

Follow-up Interviews at the End of the Pilot Year

After a year of field testing, the teacher evaluation instruments and the trial procedures must be refined. Figure 4.12 contains the teacher evaluation questions used by the SIM team to survey each evaluator and evaluatee. A similar form is used to check the effectiveness of the administrator performance evaluation system. From these suggestions and personal testimony by the field-test participants at stakeholders' meetings, the SIM consultants revise and refine the system. Typically, the number of criteria for teacher performance evaluation will be reduced and administrator performance evaluation items will be added.

Teachers generally report that they enjoy the new system and that it helps that they and their appraiser share a new, common language. Lamentably, principals often report the administrator cycle they experienced during the test-and-try year was sketchy, their evaluators did not spend enough time observing their work, and their immediate supervisor did not spend enough time on coaching and on conferences. This information from both teachers and administrators is sorted, weighed, and used to revise the system for Year Three to suggest specific training experiences for appraisers.

Year Three Training and Evaluation

The theme repeated throughout this description of the SIM approach to teacher performance evaluation is "good organizations don't just evaluate your

Figure 4.12
Survey Questions of the Test-and-Try Year

1. Each criterion is listed with two questions asked:
   a. Is this item clear?
   b. Can data be gathered from the item?
2. Should any of the criteria be deleted?
3. Is there a need to revise any of the following procedures?
   a. Preobservation conference
   b. Observation (announced)
   c. Feedback conference
   d. Supportive data and input
   e. Summative evaluation
   f. Writing professional development plans
4. Were informal performance data gathered during this time?
5. Please make any suggestions regarding the usefulness of the forms and records which are part of the Teacher Performance Evaluation system.
   a. Preobservation Data/Formative Evaluation Report
   b. Summative Evaluation Report
   c. Professional Development Plan
6. Do the forms and records seem adequate for gathering the data needed for evaluating teacher performance?
7. Do you have any suggestions for time economy during the cycle as it now exists?
8. Comments and/or General Suggestions:

competence, they train you to be more competent." Continued training of appraisers to become more effective coaches of teachers is a must. Additionally, Year Three data allows the stakeholders, cabinet, and principals to examine performance data for all personnel in all school buildings.

Next, the stakeholders committee must deal with the "yes-buts." Someone on the stakeholders' committee will say, "Yes, what we have accomplished is very good, *but* what about . . . . ?" Shoring up these weak areas in the system occupies Year Three.

Starting with the rather straightforward notion of evaluating and improving how teachers teach, we typically add the following elements:

- School climate measures to determine school effectiveness (Sweeney 1986).

- Feedback from students and parents to supplement teacher and administrator performance evaluation.

- Staff development activities targeting valleys in performance profiles of teachers and administrators.

- Student achievement reports, both norm-referenced and criterion-referenced, disaggregated by race, gender, and socioeconomic status. We stress that the most important criterion is, "Do the kids learn?"

Finally, when the stakeholders recommend it—but not before—we tackle the problem of a subroutine of the total performance evaluation—usually called intensive assistance for marginal teachers. After examining Year Three data and comparing teacher performance across departments, buildings, and the district, approximately 2-4 percent of the teaching staff will not meet district standards. Some can be helped by an employee assistance plan. Most, however, just don't teach well enough.

The Marginal Teacher

Now it is time to follow through on the due-process acronym NEAT (notice, explanation, assistance, time). Many SIM clients have provided an intensive assistance program to improve or, if all else fails, to remove marginal teachers.

The teacher performance evaluation cycle of observations, conferences, and report making is used for all teachers. Professional Improvement Commitments are written to help teachers improve deficiencies. However, if a teacher is rated below district standards on three or more criteria, a special support team will help.

CATE/S has a complete array of reports on teacher performance and access to computer-generated improvement and growth plans that can also provide the marginal teacher with assistance.

The assistance team plan is well understood by teachers, their union, the board, administrators, and the community. It is set up well in advance of a teacher "being in trouble" and is a natural outgrowth of developing a new teacher evaluation system. All teachers are eligible for the assistance provided that their performance is below standard. The purpose of assistance teams is clearly stated in a brochure that is provided to all employees and other interested parties.

The "assistance team" concept is based on procedures that are basic and should remain constant (see Figure 4.13).

- The building principal is the prime evaluator. (Nothing in the plan reduces the authority of the principal.)
- The executive directors of elementary and secondary education, their assistant directors, and the director of personnel form the evaluative support team to building principals for teacher evaluation. (All have had extensive training in the same groups. Rater reliability has been established and maintained over time).

Figure 4.13
Simultaneous Assistance Team and Evaluation Process

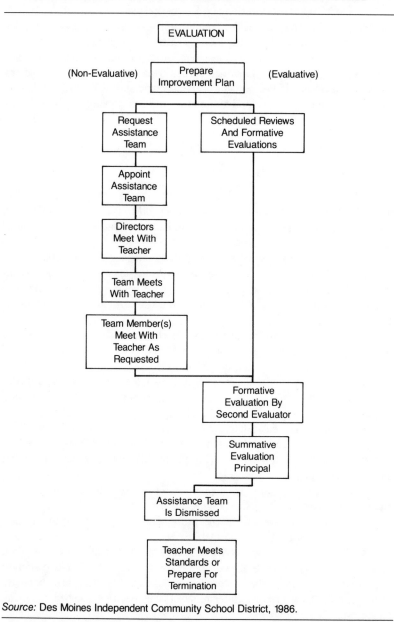

Source: Des Moines Independent Community School District, 1986.

- Content-area supervisors may become involved in the performance evaluation through the invitation of the building principal. (The entire array of supervisory contact with any teacher may be used.)
- The curriculum division is a resource to develop and extend intensive strategies.
- Intensive assistance teams (usually three people—one administrator to chair the team, a clinical supervision expert, and a subject matter specialist) work with a teacher for at least 15 days.

Both large and small districts can implement the teacher performance evaluation cycle of observations, conferences, and report making. Smaller school districts with limited resources have been able to use the same team approach using a district cadre of well-trained team members supplemented by reciprocal help from neighboring districts or free-lance consultants.

As the intensive assistance concept has developed, the SIM research team has carefully monitored the results. On the average, half of the teachers who have experienced a year of intensive assistance have improved and have been moved back to the regular teacher evaluation cycle. The other half have been dismissed. To date, there has been no litigation. Parents, teachers, and the management team of the districts agree that intensive assistance coupled to professional teacher performance evaluation works. The approach satisfies the call of Maria Johnson, the board president, for "a defensible teacher evaluation system designed not only to remove incompetent teachers but also to improve the effectiveness of all of the district's teachers."

References

Des Moines Independent Community School District. *Assistance Teams*. Des Moines, Iowa: Author, 1986.

Doyle, K. *Evaluating Teaching*. New York: D.C. Heath and Company, 1983.

Etaugh, C., and E. Foresman. "Evaluations of Competence as a Function of Sex and Marital Status." *Sex Roles* 9, 7 (July 1983): 759-765.

Garvey School District. *Certified Evaluation System*. Rosemead, Calif.: Garvey School District, June 1987.

Henderson, R. *Performance Appraisal*. Reston, Va.: Reston Publishing Company, Inc., 1984.

Hidlebaugh, E. "A Model for Developing a Teaching Performance Evaluation System: A Multiple Appraiser Approach." Doctoral diss., Iowa State University, 1973.

Ilgen, D. "Gender Issues in Performance Appraisal: A Discussion of O'Leary and Hansen." In *Performance Measurement and Theory*, edited by F. Landy, S. Zedek, and J. Cleveland. Hillsdale, N.J.: Lawrence Erlbaum Associates, 1983.

Iowa Department of Education. *Standards for Approval of Training Programs for Teacher Evaluators*. Des Moines, Iowa: Department of Education, 1987.

Joint Committee on the Standards for Educational Evaluation. "Standards for Evaluation of Educational Personnel" (first draft), edited by Daniel Stuffehearn. Kalamazoo, Mich.: Evaluation Center, Western Michigan University, January 1986.

Landy, F., and J. Farr. "Performance Rating." *Psychological Bulletin* 87 (January 1980): 72-107.

Manatt, R. P. "Staff Development, School Improvement, and a Microcomputer." *Journal of Staff Development* (in progress).

Manatt, R. P., W. Hawana, J. Mitchell, R. Schlotfeldt, S. Stow, and L. Stevenson. *Operator's Manual for Computer Assisted Teacher Evaluation/Supervision (CATE/S)*. Ames: Iowa State University Research Foundation, 1986.

Manatt, R. P., K. Palmer, and E. Hidlebaugh. "Evaluating Teacher Performance With Improved Rating Scales." *NASSP Bulletin* 60, 401 (September 1976): 21-24.

Manatt, R. P., and S. B. Stow. *The Clinical Manual for Teacher Performance Evaluation*. Ames: Iowa State University Research Foundation, 1984.

Manatt, R. P., and S. Stow. *Developing and Testing a Model for Measuring and Improving Educational Outcomes of K-12 Schools: Technical Report*. Ames: Iowa State University, February 1986.

Peterson, D. "Rating Teacher Performance to Determine Career Ladder Advancement: An Analysis of Bias and Reliability." Doctoral diss., Iowa State University, (in press).

Pulakos, E. "A Comparison of Rater Training Programs: Error Training and Accuracy Training." *Journal of Applied Psychology* 69, 4 (November 1984): 581-88.

Redfern, G. *Evaluating Teachers and Administrators: A Performance Objectives Approach*. Boulder, Colo.: Westview Press, Inc., 1980.

School Improvement Model Office. *The School Improvement Model Kit*. Ames, Iowa: Author, 1987.

Stow, S. B. "Writing Professional Improvement Commitments—A Skill That Can Be Taught." *Journal of the Illinois Association for Supervision and Curriculum Development* (in press).

Stow, S.B., R.P. Manatt, J. Mitchell, and W. Hawana. *Compendium of Validated Professional Improvement Commitments*, vol. 2. Ames: Iowa State University Research Foundation, 1987.

Stow, S.B., and J.E. Sweeney. "Developing a Teacher Performance Evaluation System." *Educational Leadership* 38 (April 1981): 538-541.

Strahan, R. "More on Averaging Judges' Ratings: Determining the Most Reliable Composite." *Journal of Consulting and Clinical Psychology* 48, 5 (October 1980): 587-589.

Sweeney, J. E. "Developing A Strong Climate: The Key to School Improvement." *National Forum of Educational Administration and Supervision* 3, 3 (1986) 234-143.

Wexley, K., and Yukl. *Organizational Behavior and Personnel Psychology*. Homewood, Ill.: Richard D. Irwin, Inc., 1984.

Wise, A. E., L. Darling-Hammond, M. W. McLaughlin, and H. T. Bernstein. *Teacher Evaluation: A Study of Effective Practices*. Santa Monica, Calif.: Rand Corporation, 1984.

LOREN E. SANCHEZ

From the Practitioner's Point of View...

Manatt's response to Superintendent Jergens' request for an effective, consistent teacher evaluation program is a comprehensive approach to putting together a performance management system. Joining improvement and accountability goals into a single evaluation system is practical and workable, although certain skills need to be developed for each component. I agree with Manatt that the initial focus of evaluation is not on dismissing an employee, but on helping teachers and administrators enhance their performance. An additional function would be to modify teachers' and administrators' capacities to change their behaviors and attitudes.

The process of developing a system is critical. Option #4 allows the stakeholders to create ownership, provided that certain conditions exist: mutual trust between teachers and administrators, a commitment to self and organizational renewal, and a stable environment. Beyond that, involvement of those outside the stakeholder group assures good communication.

Monitoring the performance management system is important to ensure the maximum professional growth of each teacher. District administrators have a major responsibility for monitoring site administrators by assuring congruence between the teacher's performance and the written evaluation. This involves district personnel knowing what is going on in schools and classrooms and discussing with the principal each teacher's performance, and the principal's efforts to help all teachers grow. District personnel also need to read the written evaluations of all teachers and provide feedback to the site administrators.

All teachers and administrators need to be evaluated *each* year, not every other year. And supervision and evaluation need to be differentiated for each teacher depending on his or her specific performance and attitude.

The amount of paperwork and various forms in Manatt's approach seems excessive. It has been my experience that you must find a happy medium in the amount of required paperwork, including necessary documentation.

The amount and quality of training for any system is crucial. Inservice in goal setting, conferencing, supervision, instruction, curricular areas, interpersonal skills, conflict management, educational change, and organizational theory and development provides an ongoing training agenda for teachers and administrators. From what we know about effective training, it is clear that a good evaluation system requires a substantial investment of time for all concerned.

Effective evaluation of teachers and administrators enhances the educational program for students while advancing the skills of staff members. The process must be taken seriously if it is to produce positive and long-lasting effects on a school district.

Loren E. Sanchez, recently appointed Superintendent of the Upland (California) Unified School District, has been a classroom teacher, principal, director of instructional programs, and an assistant/associate superintendent.

5 Evaluating Teachers as Professionals: The Duties-Based Approach

MICHAEL SCRIVEN

The system proposed here is intended to be practical and valid, but there is some tension between these two requirements. In essence, it costs a little more to have a valid system. Most of the components are tried and true; the system's novelty lies in the exclusion of the usual invalid elements and the inclusion of enough valid ones to provide an adequate foundation for personnel decisions including appointment, tenure, retention, and the opposite of each. It treats teachers as responsible professionals who retain a great deal of autonomy in the way they discharge their duties. This implies that they acknowledge the need for accountability and systematic professional development, each of which requires an evaluation process. It also implies that they should expect, and get, full protection from an evaluation system that is arbitrary, invalid, unnecessarily intrusive, unjust, or unable to provide useful information.[1]

Michael Scriven is Professor of Education, University of Western Australia, Nedlands.

[1]This is a discussion of the evaluation of teachers in the primary and secondary schools, but essentially similar principles apply to post-secondary teachers; the major difference is the weighting of the non-classroom obligation to do research.

Preliminaries

Before looking at a valid approach, we will first consider my reasons for concluding that alternative approaches are untenable. Unless this point is convincingly established, there is no reason to make the effort to set up a new system. First, however, we need to look at a number of related background issues.

Teaching as a Profession

One such issue is whether teaching is in fact a profession. No assumption is made here that it is or is not a profession in the full sense of the term. It is clear that many teachers behave like professionals and that many others do not. Still, individual teachers and some of their subject matter associations do accept a general responsibility for keeping up to date on content and to some extent on pedagogy, one of the most critical features of the professions.[2] And there is no doubt that, like the typical professional, the teacher works in an environment where many of the obligations of the job are understood rather than spelled out in a job description. For these and other reasons, a model of evaluation appropriate to the professions is the only model that is both feasible and valid for the evaluation of teaching.

The Limits of Negotiation

Another factor affecting teacher evaluation is the political situation, including existing collective bargaining agreements. Since political conditions vary from state to state, from public to private school systems, and from district to district, there is little discussion here about political compromises, although they must be addressed.

---

[2]Teachers have to consider both advantages and disadvantages about being treated as professionals. Representatives of industrial unions often deride the professionalism thesis as a way to get more work out of teachers without any more pay. An alternative and often-voiced view is that there is very little chance of teachers getting significantly better pay scales—in many districts—without some corresponding increase in professionalism. Such complaints are often supported by suggesting that real professionals would exhibit more concern with getting the job done well than with minimizing the hours of work. For example, it is difficult to reconcile professionalism with the insistence that inservice training occur during the school year at the expense of student learning time, instead of during the summer; or with pushing for the granting of tenure after over-short probationary periods, instead of relating it to the time it takes to make a sound decision.

Dismal though the status of teaching may be at the college level, it is at least true that a seven-year probationary period is still generally applied, whereas schools are moving towards one year (a nominal two years often amount to one if the advanced warning requirements are stringent). Teachers themselves often say that it took them four or five years to develop even a sense of confidence, and many say that a sense of mastery only came in the seventh to tenth year.

Discussing any proposed evaluation system with teachers or their representatives often leads to improvements that benefit all parties. Teachers must be treated as legitimately concerned employees who will be significantly affected by a proposal; in return, teachers must acknowledge administrators' concerns with ensuring accountability and optimizing student benefits and staff competence.

There is a special problem with compromises that have resulted in contracts or conditions of work that incorporate improper, invalid, or inadequate procedures. Excluding all consideration of student performance from teacher evaluation procedures, requiring evaluation to be based on a few prearranged classroom visits, or prohibiting review of teachers who are not applying for a promotion or raise are examples of such errors. These conditions should be negotiated out as soon as possible because they avoid full accountability and professionalism. The aim of schools is to provide the best service to students and community. There is no room in that formula for any party to avoid accountability or professional development.

Administrator Accountability

A major theme of my approach to teacher evaluation is accountability, which might be summarized as "responsibility includes demonstrability." But for a school system to show responsible use of its resources it must evaluate its use of each of the various components.

Accountability is best seen as a property of whole systems rather than of subsystems. It is difficult to enforce much accountability on one subsystem if you can't tell how much of what happens there is due to deficiencies in some other subsystem that is *not* being checked. In particular, there can be no full accountability of teachers without accountability of administrators. This is partly because teachers' efficiency depends on how administrators provide services (i.e., dealing with troublemakers). Also, it is ethically objectionable to expect teachers to commit to an evaluation that administrators avoid, because administrators need it just as much and the community has the same right to it. Hence, this discussion of teacher evaluation assumes that there is a sound process of administrator evaluation in place or being put in place.

The Connection to Professional Development

While not an imperative to quite the same degree as the need to have a serious system for supporting personnel decisions, it is desirable and often politically important for a system of teacher evaluation to include an improvement component. (A core system provides only for summative evaluation; an enriched system provides both formative and summative evaluation.)

Sometimes, the best summative process will spin off useful formative insights. But recommendations for improvement in teaching typically require more detailed diagnostic evaluation and a different kind of knowledge than personnel decisions, just as prescriptions for treating a serious illness require more careful examination, testing, and knowledge than needed to determine that the patient is seriously ill.

The claim that opens this section is very carefully phrased. It should be sharply distinguished from the oft-made statement that systems of teacher evaluation should be aimed at improvement rather than at personnel decisions; or the claim that negative judgments about competence are invalid unless backed up by a list of specific recommendations that, if followed, would produce acceptable performance. You might as well argue that you cannot validly conclude that typists have failed a typing test unless you can work out a training formula for getting them through it. The task of personnel evaluation is to evaluate the performance of personnel; the task of training or development is to alter behavior so that it meets minimum standards of performance.

Providing remediation is highly desirable from the employees' point of view, but it is an enterprise beyond developing a valid system for justifying personnel decisions, and it goes beyond what is provided for most professional and industrial workers. Essentially, the school board must decide if it is appropriate to spend the extra money for a system of detailed diagnosis and remediation rather than replace incompetent teachers. (The evidence suggests that it is more expensive to remediate.) Educational practice has been to go for an enriched system of teacher and administrator evaluation. And if a new system of personnel evaluation is being introduced, then fairness requires provision for remediation since the rules are being changed. But once a changeover has occurred, a fair system of summative evaluation does not have to be an enriched system.

Notice the crucial difference between the two absolute requirements that apply to a system of personnel evaluation, and the one that does not. The courts and the unions have frequently confused them.

1. It is absolutely necessary that there be solid evidence for any negative conclusion[3] on which an adverse personnel action is based; and this evidence should go beyond the judgment of one person, however experienced or well-credentialed.[4]

---

[3]The focus on negative conclusions is simply because these are the job-threatening ones and hence the most serious for all concerned; the logic is just the same when justifying award conclusions.

[4]To a layman's eye, the courts' line of thought suggests that it might be enough for a single person to have witnessed several serious transgressions; it isn't enough for the case to rest on the interpretation (judgment) of a single person and it may not be enough for it to rest on the judgments of several such people, if the amount of judgment is considerable or of debatable validity.

2. It is essential that negative conclusions identify the details of the deficiency in performance. For example, one who fails a typing test should be told the extent to which the failure was due to speed deficiency and accuracy deficiency. Where several dimensions are involved, their relative weight should also be specified, and it should be stated whether there are scores below which deficiencies cannot be traded off by scoring high on other dimensions.

3. It is not relevant to the validity, demonstrability, or fairness of a personnel evaluation to identify either the cause of the deficiency or a set of procedures which, if followed, would eliminate it.

Another way to bring out the difference between legitimate and illegitimate demands on the evaluation system is expressed in the italicized words of the following sentence: "While the system proposed here and most of the invalid systems currently in place readily spin off *directions* along which one needs to move for improvement (that is, the dimensions of the deficiency—along with its magnitude) from which one can easily *infer* in *most* cases how to go about *improving* one's performance, that is very different from providing a *guaranteed* and *comprehensive* remediation procedure, let alone the kind of *support and training* that will ensure success *at the time of the final review.*"

Teaching ability is situation specific. It should never be argued that because some teachers are not very good with 12th grade history students (or retarded 8th grade students in a history course, or graduate students in a history seminar) that they are not good teachers or even not good history teachers. There are plenty of counterexamples to that kind of overgeneralization. Conversely, it should never be assumed that a teacher with an outstanding track record elsewhere or in earlier years can be brought up to acceptable standards in every teaching job. Some teachers are simply not suitable and never will be suitable for a particular job within their field of certification. (There is a close analogy with the tasks of research and acting.)

Hence it is absurd to suggest that an evaluator must always be able to indicate how a person could become a good teacher in a current situation. The appropriate requirement is simply that the evaluator be able to indicate the dimensions and magnitude of the deficiency. Any more than that must come from someone with remediation knowledge and skills.

Segregating Summative Evaluation from Development Support

The Ideal. In a system that includes remediation support, several components should be fully segregated from the summative evaluation: results of a formative evaluation, recommendations for learning/training/practice, and observations on progress. Without this separation, it is unreasonable to expect teachers to go to formative advisers about their weaknesses. One might as well expect clients to seek advice from attorneys who are doubling as judges on the same case. Furthermore, teachers getting help from the person who will judge them is akin to teaching to the test or authors reviewing their own works. It is a poor way to ensure objective evaluation, but it has been the norm for decades.

Separating the roles does not have to involve great expense in larger schools, since it mainly involves a different way of slicing the administrative workload. In most systems, the principal, who makes and defends the personnel decisions (even if they have to be approved by the superintendent and sometimes the board), is the natural choice to be the summative evaluator. In some school systems, an assistant principal can then be put in charge of the support system.

There are advantages, however, to using an outside consultant as a formative evaluator—and it may not be much more costly. Also, using an outside consultant reduces the likelihood of the support person accidentally revealing confidential information or having to refuse a superior's improper request for confidential information.

Credibility is advanced by using "mentor teachers"—outstanding teachers in the same or another school—in the formative evaluator's role. The mentor position is an appointment that requires serious evaluation and pays off in increased salary and prestige. No matter who plays the staff development role—principal, consultant, or mentor—the adequacy of that person's performance should be rated almost exclusively by the teachers served.

The Reality. Isn't all this too squeamish? After all, the practice of having supervisors make summative recommendations on their supervisees, as well as helping them improve, is widespread in the helping professions. Teachers and parents have to serve in both the summative and formative modes for children. Isn't it part of the human condition to have to cope with multiple roles?

Of course it is, but it leads to poor performance in many situations and should be avoided if possible. The key question is how much the school system is interested in improving current staff performance. If seriously interested, it has to deal with the fact that many teachers won't go to a principal for help because it is likely to disadvantage them, and they don't like to go to their peers or can't get help from them.

The counselor/judge conflict has spawned many responses but no solutions. In the academic area, we have long used external exams as a way to free teachers to be allies with students in the common cause of success on exams. Parents have often divided the disciplinary and the supportive role between them, or between them and the school.

In the professions, we often allow a period of apprenticeship when close supervision is essential and professional or personal rivalry is scarcely relevant. During that period we try to provide at least some independent assessment, but we usually move toward a different approach as autonomy develops.

We look for objective measures of performance—the postmortem and the organ committee for the doctor, the publications list for the researcher, the ratio of successes in court for the attorney. In schools we have failed to do this. The usual concession to the experienced teacher is to make classroom visits perfunctory, or to omit them entirely. This deprives the teacher of what should be valuable information.[5] It also deprives the community of the improved teaching that should result from regular evaluation and insurance against keeping teachers who are no longer doing an acceptable job.

Practical Compromises. If we wish to improve teaching, we need to bring the reality closer to the ideal. If resources will not permit a division of labor or the use of consultants or mentors, then we must simply do the best we can to help the principal separate the roles internally. Some steps in that direction are:

• Using standardized forms on which only legitimate dimensions are rated.

• Holding staff meetings a few times a year at which the principal can express views without putting pressure on individuals to do what he or she says. (What the principal likes is not necessarily the same as what the job requires.)

• Providing strict training for all principals in the difference between what they can legitimately observe in a classroom and what they must disregard.

• Providing good print or courseware resources for teachers and a subsidy for attending inservice seminars so they can get frank advice externally.

• Providing audio and video recorders so that teachers can evaluate themselves.

• Rewarding teachers explicitly for helping peers.

Teacher Competency Testing vs. Teacher Evaluation

The most important need in the schools is for a comprehensive approach to teacher evaluation. Nevertheless, some piecemeal approaches have value. Properly used, they can avoid some major disasters for students and schools,

---

[5]The idea that teachers benefit from regular summative evaluation is often thought to be naive or deceptive. Far from it. Although one hears the complaint often enough in the U.S., it is striking how many teachers in Western Australia who volunteered submissions to the Beazley Committee in 1983 lamented the fact that in 20 years no one have ever bothered to visit their classroom, or talk about their problems and questions about teaching. What are we telling such teachers? We may think that we are telling them that we trust them; but since everyone knows that some of the long-term teachers are complete disasters, what we are really telling them is that we don't care enough about the education of students or the professional development of teachers to check on the process.

and they can be put in place quickly, fairly, and cheaply. Fast and cheap is no substitute for fair and full, but it is sometimes better than nothing.

Some of the most popular piecemeal plans are related to tests of minimum competence in basic skills, knowledge of subject matter, and pedagogy. Of these, the last one raises some serious problems. A major effort was made a number of years ago to base teacher education curriculums on a complete set of pedagogical competencies (competency-based teacher education).[6] It turned out to be somewhat ahead of the research of its time and not a useful basis for overall teacher appraisal.

But there are areas of pedagogy in which the proper use of research is less debatable. Test-construction and test-interpretation skills and minimum competence in the use of simple audiovisual devices—and perhaps even of computers—might be candidates for testing. This is not because every teacher should use all of these skills, but because everyone should know how to use them to be able to take advantage of their special benefits. (The development of more sophisticated competency tests by the Carnegie Project at Stanford can be expected to increase our repertoire in both quality and quantity.) In the end, however, competency testing can only provide a partial approach to evaluation. One must have a great deal more, such as input from students and parents.

But the first point to make about the logic of such tests is that they can only be used to support unfavorable actions. There is nothing unfair about this, though teachers often claim that there is. Good secretaries are more than good typists, but no one ever suggested that makes it unfair to use a typing test as a screening test. The same logic applies at mid-career; there is much more to being a good surgeon than good diagnosis, but no one ever suggested we should keep surgeons on staff who keep removing healthy organs.

Competency tests must be a valid way to identify the presence of a minimum level of knowledge or skill that is essential for competent teaching. They must also be applied uniformly to all for whom they are relevant and can only be selected from a range of such tests on grounds that preempt deliberate discrimination.

By failing to test all the other dimensions of good teaching, the competency approach fails as a procedure for identifying good teachers. But if it does test one minimum level of competency on one dimension, it can screen out people who should not be in the profession at all. Their deficiency in this

---

[6]Some comments on the approach will be found in "Evaluating Program Effectiveness or, If the Program is Competency Based, How Come the Evaluation is Costing So Much?" ERIC Document No. SP008 235 (ED 093866), in *Research in Education*, November 1974.

dimension cannot be made up by their performance on other dimensions, so the fact that performance on the other dimensions is not tested is irrelevant to the validity of using the test.

The adequacy of competency testing needs separate consideration. A test of teacher literacy that is perfectly valid in principle may be used in a way that provides no insurance against incompetence. If, for example, the cutting score for passing is set too low (as in Texas), or if unlimited retesting is allowed despite the existence of only a small pool of items (as in Florida), then incompetent teachers will get through.

Pro-Teacher vs. Pro-Administrator Evaluation Systems

Those of us who have proposed systems for teacher evaluation are often asked if the system is "pro-teacher" or "pro-administrator" (the latter being taken to mean anti-teacher). And no doubt we all respond by saying that it is neutral. The approach taken here is balanced on several points. On the one hand, the system provides a very strong defense of the teacher against unjust evaluation methods, which include virtually all current approaches. Furthermore, this system insists on the complete right of teachers as professionals to select the approach to teaching that best suits their own character, talents, students, subject matter, and, once tenured, right to disregard without penalty suggestions for improvement from their superiors. This approach argues for a strong support system that is segregated from the summative, the first requirement being a way to eliminate a very important source of injustice.

Also, the approach taken here provides a very strong defense of the student, parent, and taxpayer against exploitation by the lazy or incompetent teacher. Among other things, this system completely rejects the idea of resting teacher evaluation mainly on peer assessments, or on the assumption that someone who was once competent is forever competent, or on a request for promotion, or on the ability to specify remediation procedures, or on the overall, undetailed judgment of a principal who may be weak or a crony. It defends the right of the teacher to disregard the principal's advice, but it does nothing to soften the need to meet the standard.

The Need for a New System

We need a new system because all the old ones are inefficient, invalid, and unjust. Even the systems built into the latest handbooks for teacher evaluation are illegitimate. If the arguments presented here are correct, we will have to expect that most existing systems will be thrown out by the courts, raising the possibility of colossal retroactive damages.

The first target is the latest and apparently most respectable approach, "research-based teacher evaluation." It is best to begin with this one because its advocates are already convinced of the inadequacy of the other approaches. However, if it can be shown that this new approach does not work, then it is appropriate to reexamine the others as well. We have a great deal of experience with them, so if one of them can be salvaged, we should use it instead of switching to a completely new system.

Research-Based Teacher Evaluation

One cannot use in personnel evaluation any of the research on teaching that has allegedly shown certain teaching styles[7] to be more effective than others. It had been supposed that this research meant we could use classroom visits to see which teachers best exemplify these winning styles—and use the results of those observations to select, promote, or retain better teachers—but we cannot use any such observations in any such way.

The essential problem is not that the generalizations aren't true.[8] To understand the real problem, we should start with a case where we have learned to appreciate the impropriety of using empirically sound generalizations in personnel decisions.

Considerations of Justice. Let us suppose that it is true that women tend, statistically speaking, to make better primary school teachers than men. That fact would not justify using gender in selecting an applicant for a post as a primary school teacher. It is not that using gender is a violation of affirmative action or that it would be politically unpopular with men. The fundamental reason is that selection for jobs by gender is simply a violation of natural justice. It involves guilt by association, penalizing people because of the average performance of a group to which they belong instead of judging them on their own merit. Even if women are 50 times more likely than men to make good primary teachers, you must base your decision solely on the legal credentials and track record of each candidate.

---

[7]The concept of style as it is used here can best be defined by example. The styles of teaching that RBTE usually favors include the use of advance organizers (lesson objectives put on the board, handed out, or mentioned); asking questions of students, encouraging students to ask questions; frequently providing positive reinforcement, maintaining eye contact; and maintaining high time on task. The failure to employ or exhibit any or all of these is also a style. On the other hand, treating students justly, providing them with feedback on their academic progress, explaining material in language they can understand, and giving them clear directions about assignments, are not matters of style. They are duties.

[8]Although there are some complaints that they involve illicit generalization from small studies to other regions, student types, and subject matters. But there is also a problem about the definition of good teaching that many of them involve, since it frequently omits long-term retention measures and performance on out-of-class duties.

We all have some feeling for that point when it's applied to gender, racial, or religious discrimination, but it applies equally to all personnel decisions made on the basis of any generalization about a group, including the group that teaches in a certain way. Any use of evidence about an individual's teaching style, as opposed to teaching achievement, is a violation of natural justice.

Considerations of Efficiency. Of course, if the correlations between gender and merit are extremely high and if it is very expensive to get or interpret track record data on individuals, it might be more costly to follow the path of justice.[9] Nevertheless, we would have to get track record data for the same reason we pay the bill for public defenders—because justice outranks economy. In fact, the correlations we are talking about are modest; they cannot be combined to obtain higher correlations (because we have no reason to think them statistically independent of each other, the precondition for amalgamation). For the most part, we already have or can easily get the track record data. So the special cases in which you might try to justify using the generalizations to save money or time do not apply. The simple truth is that track record data are better predictors than any others.

But can't we at least use *both* kinds of data—simply combine the track record data with the style data? No, it's still unjust, since it makes part of the judgment dependent on data that aren't about the individual candidate. These two types of data are not statistically independent and hence can't be combined. Possessing the track record data automatically makes the other

---

[9]It all depends on how you estimate the costs of mistakes vs. the benefits of success. The problem is that the costs are different if one calculates them from the point of view of the administrator or the point of view of the applicants, the children, or the taxpayers. For the administrator, it is very stressful to have to open with the complaints about a bad teacher, and possibly with the enormous effort involved in trying to dismiss with cause. So the administrator tends to clutch at straws that might reduce what he or she sees as bad choices. Technically, this is the effort to reduce false positives. By contrast, passing over a good teacher (because he or she happens to have a style that is not typical of good teachers) doesn't show up as a cost to the administrator—unless no candidates pass the Approved Style Test. In fact, missing a good teacher is just as much a bad choice, just as much an error, a false negative. It's just that the cost is not paid by the administrator. It will be paid by the candidate who doesn't get the job and by the students who will not get the best teacher.

One key point for the administrator to remember is that as long as the other administrators are using the Approved Style Test (AST), a strong competitive advantage is gained by ignoring it, since the pool that is passed over will contain some and possibly all of the best candidates if you are prepared to judge them on their own merit. Remember that those not prejudiced against the award of post doctoral fellowships to women finished up with better scholars, and the same was true with stock analysts, news directors, and airline pilots. Of course, it has to be shown that using the AST does not give an advantage, and that's what this section is about.

generalization irrelevant, because the overall generalization refers to *random* samples from a certain defined population, and what you know about the candidates shows they are *not* random samples from that population.

Using the generalization is akin to buying a used Honda Civic without driving it on the grounds that the road tests identify it as the best car in its class. That's just bad practice, and it's a bad scientific method since you fail to get evidence that you could easily gather, evidence that would greatly increase the chance of making a successful prediction.

Considerations of Scientific Method. The key point here is that scientific method covers data gathering, not just data processing. You are just as guilty of using poor scientific method when you don't get evidence that's obviously relevant as when you draw the wrong inference from the evidence you do have.

A doctor who decides not to call for a biopsy on a chest lump in a male patient because it's statistically unlikely for males to get breast cancer is guilty of scientific error. Making personnel decisions on the basis of style generalizations is exactly the same.

The First Underlying Fallacy. Our thinking about such matters has been careless because of two attractive oversimplifications. The first fallacy is the supposition that the error underlying discrimination is an error of fact. We have become accustomed to rejecting discrimination against women candidates for school administration positions on the simple grounds there's no evidence they are inferior. That appears to be the case, but in a sense it's the easy way out. It doesn't matter whether they are inferior; that would still be no justification for the discrimination. It's perfectly evident that some women are better administrators than some men, just as the reverse is true. That alone means you have to look at the individual cases. That's what justice requires. Science requires the same, though it's less easy to see this point.

Even if no women were better administrators than any men, you still couldn't use gender as an indicator, because the evidence for such generalizations necessarily refers to past cases, and you can't assume that it will be true of the next case you run into. The cultural and media environments change, consciousness changes, laws and training programs change, women change, men change, jobs change. Any generalizations about the relative merit of men and women for certain jobs that happen to be true at any moment are only historical summaries, not a usable basis for future decisions.

The Second Fallacy. Many people feel that we should never throw out statistically invalid indicators because they always tell us at least part of the truth. From this there arises some of the resentment one often finds about civil rights or affirmative action legislation, which denies the right to use gender or race as discriminators. But statistical generalizations do not tell us part of the truth; they tell us all that is known about some variables in a situation where all that we know is the value of some other variables.

In the situation in which all we know about two candidates is their gender, then the whole of the truth about their teaching ability in primary school is that the women are more likely to be good at it than the men. If all that we know about two candidates is their race, then the whole of the truth about their criminal record is that the black candidate is more likely to be a criminal than the white one.

The catch with this kind of knowledge is that it is totally conditional. It only exists if the conditions are met. The moment you know something else about the candidates, it is in jeopardy. Thus, if you know that all the candidates have college degrees, you no longer know that the blacks are more likely to have criminal records because college education markedly affects incidents of criminality. With teachers, the research on winning styles tells you that if all you know about two teachers is that one exhibits a winning style and the other does not, the one with the winning style is more likely to be successful. The dilemma is this: If you also know something about their track record, you've violated the cognition of ignorance about any other relevant data, so the style generalization no longer applies. And if you don't know anything about their track records, you have violated the condition of conscientious performance of your own duties. In short, the use of style data justifies only one kind of personnel decision—the dismissal of the person who uses it.

Style Data as a Contaminant

The preceding warnings are not just about guarding against a small source of error in a procedure that is mostly acceptable. There is also the problem of invalidating all of an approach that involves even one appeal to a statistical indicator. The reasoning is the same as that which invalidates personnel interviews in which candidates are asked questions about their private lives. Even if 99 percent of the information acquired is licit, the response to the 1 item that is illicit may in fact be very influential in the decision. This can be so even if no one present thinks it was influential and even its official weighting on the personnel forms was slight or zero. The involvement of illicit indicators contaminates the whole process because you can't prove they were ignored.

Measurement-Based Teacher Evaluation

The most obvious alternative, one which also appears to offer some of the objectivity of science, is to replace indicators of success with direct measures of learning by the students. In special cases this can lead to a usable result, and the courts have shown that they will accept such approaches. But they are relatively rare. The fundamental problem with this approach is that the measures simply provide raw data about something that is happening while the teacher is teaching. To get an evaluative conclusion, one must establish causality and have some validated standards to apply the data. The standards must be supported by proof that this much achievement by these students (in this school, in this subject, with this much background, and this amount of parental support) represents a very good achievement by the teacher—or very poor achievement, or somewhere in between.

Even if we have comparative data about how much the students of different teachers in the same school have learned, based on common tests of a common curriculum, tests that are designed, administered, and scored independently of all the teachers, and even if the classes are matched for pretest ability and intelligence, we still can't tell whether any of the teachers are competent or brilliant. We can only tell how they stand on relative competence. But comparative conclusions really won't justify most personnel decisions. For example, they won't justify decisions about retention and tenure; the worst of a group of teachers may be good, the best may be poor. Strictly speaking, you shouldn't fire people for relative incompetence, nor should you give them tenure or promotion for relative competence.[10] Thus, we have to do more than obtain evidence of comparative learning gains as part of the relevant evidence.

Apart from the fact that the best conclusions you can get from comparative learning gain scores aren't the ones you really need, it is extremely difficult to meet the conditions mentioned. There are other, fundamental, worries about the measurement alternative. For example, it is a major problem that, in its usual form, measurement doesn't attend to content, only to learning gains. Measurement is quantitative, but not qualitative, and we need both. Substantial aspects of the content or its interpretation are usually under the control of the teacher and should surely be evaluated. After all, teaching rests on the value of the content for almost its entire justification. And then there's the matter of improper process—injustice in the classroom. There's nothing about that in the learning gain scores.

One reason we can't ignore learning gain scores completely is that we can use them, rather than teacher estimates of them, as an indication of how much a particular category of students could learn. If we don't know how much students could have learned, we can hardly complain or exclaim about how much they did learn. The extent to which an individual teacher has achieved the potentiality of the students, which is surely a measure of good teaching, can partly be inferred from students' achievements under several

---

[10]Nevertheless, a U.S. Circuit Court of Appeal has accepted the plausible argument that if two competent but not extraordinary teachers can get their students to a certain standard, a third teacher whose students come nowhere near that standard is prima facie incompetent; that is, in the absence of specific evidence to the contrary, the conclusion stands.

teachers. Thus we certainly can learn something useful from learning gains, but we can't learn everything we need from the outcome data—and we often can't get them. This approach is not a general solution to the practical problem of finding a teacher evaluation system.

The Judgment-Based Approach

It is generally thought that we should put the task of teacher evaluation into the hands of experienced teachers—or ex-teachers such as school principals. Let them directly inspect the classroom. Surely the classroom is the best source of data on how well teachers teach, and surely these people are the best judges of good teaching? Of course, they might be good judges, but how would we ever know? For that matter, how would they know? They might be overly kind in their judgments of other teachers, overly harsh, or overly affected by personal appearance or considerations of style. The standards they use might vary enormously from subject to subject, school to school, year to year as the individual or the committee membership varies. If you use judges, you have to validate them—or face the skepticism of the kind of judges you run into in court. Courts are more forgiving about the judgmental approach than they should be, probably because it is the traditional approach, and better alternatives—and the details of the failings of the judgmental approach—have not been presented.

One concern regarding teachers or principals as evaluators is that they have their own way of coping with classes and may find it difficult to accept the idea that alternative ways are every bit as good.

A further concern is that the usual number of classroom visits is far too small to provide a statistically adequate sample of what everyone knows to be a time-dependent process. Also, the sample cannot be random because the visitor's presence introduces changes of unknown magnitude. There is the possibility of social/personal bias, and the evaluator's subject-matter expertise is likely to be limited. Most of these considerations are enough by themselves to rule out the use of classroom visits as a significant basis for teacher evaluation.

The track record of peer evaluation must also be mentioned. It has turned out to be extraordinarily difficult to get peers to turn in negative evaluations. This difficulty has been encountered outside education, in the armed forces for example. Only in the very best institutions of higher education does this system work well, and then usually only because it is focused on research performance rather than on teaching.[11] The problem has been

---

[11]John Centra reports that even Carnegie-Mellon University couldn't make it work for the evaluation of teaching "Colleagues as Raters of Classroom Instruction." *Journal of Higher Education* (1975): 327-337.

called the "secret contract bias." All who are called on to make judgments are conscious of the fact that they will be on the receiving end of these judgments on another occasion. The understanding of the secret contract— not entirely implicit if a union is involved—is that if the evaluator goes easy on the victims this time around, the favor will be returned on a later occasion.

The use of principals and teachers to make judgments about teacher performance, then, is not a valid approach. However, there is a group of judges who are ready, willing, and able to assist in the process of teacher evaluation. These are the students themselves, who are in the best place of anyone to tell us some important things. For example, how well was the subject matter made comprehensible to them?[12] Given a modest amount of proper training about the evaluation of teachers, something of considerable value to them for other reasons, students from the intermediate years upward appear to be able to provide this kind of information quite well.

A Valid Alternative

The Duties-Based Approach

To find a fully adequate teacher evaluation procedure, we need to go back to fundamentals and ask two questions. What is a teacher hired to do and how can we decide whether it has been done adequately or with excellence? The teacher's primary duty is to teach students worthwhile knowledge[13] (cognitive, affective, or psychomotor, depending on the teacher's responsibilities) to the extent of the students' abilities.[14] Of course, this is normally

---

[12]One can't validate the use of student ratings on the (true) grounds that the ratings correlate with learning gains. That just gives us one more statistical indicator, as invalid as the rest. There are half a dozen other ways to validate student ratings, however, centering around the fact that students are direct observers of their own comprehension or lack of it. See "The Validity of Student Ratings" in *Instructional Evaluation* 1, 1988.

[13]Sometimes the content of the curriculum that a teacher is required to teach is not worthwhile or not deemed so by the teacher. An example would be teaching creationism as a reasonable alternative to evolutionary theory as required in some southern states. The teaching is then an undesirable duty. It still continues to be a duty as long as what is being taught is not so evil or damaging or so rigidly required that the teacher should abandon the job rather than continue to teach this material or ignore the requirement (anti-Semitism in Nazi Germany, for example).

[14]This is (sometimes) ideally done by inspiring students to enjoy the process of learning the material and of learning in general. Since that is not always possible given the constraints of entering attitudes, time, and resources, it cannot be part of the primary duty. But it might be argued that it is a duty to try this, where possible, rather than assuming it is impossible. Similarly, while it may be ideal to encourage students to learn to manage their own learning process, and hence something we should spend some time teaching them, it is not a substitute for the primary duty, which is to teach students the substantial content of the curriculum.

understood to imply satisfactory performance in the classroom, but it also entails an obligation to perform a number of tasks that are not part of the central classroom process, such as correcting homework and keeping up to date with subject matter, pedagogy, and student needs. There are many secondary duties not required to perform the primary duties, such as talking to parents, supervising corridors or lunchrooms, doing committee work, submitting information on student performance to the school administration, and referring students to appropriate counselors. These duties vary to some extent from site to site, but there are usually a good many of them that all teachers understand to be part of the job. They may be secondary but they are not dispensable; they are simply ancillary.

The duties-based approach identifies all of these tasks, uses multiple measures to get a best estimate of the extent to which they have been done well, and synthesizes the results. It never uses style indicators; it never relies on judges for anything they can't ably analyze; and it never confuses comparative merit with criterion-referenced merit. The validity of the duties-based approach derives from one source: the obligation of the employee to discharge the duties of the job to the extent that is reasonably possible with the resources available.[15] This source is unimpeachable on logical, legal, and ethical grounds.

Duties-based evaluation can be done exhaustively, in which case it is extremely time-consuming and intrusive; or it can be done pragmatically, in which case its costs are manageable and the results still valid. Nevertheless, it does take more time than the present superficial approach, which is legally and scientifically unsound. We should resign ourselves to the fact that we are going to have to put somewhat more resources into staff evaluation and development. Personnel evaluation and development is, after all, the most crucial aspect of quality control in the school, and the most important substantial task of the school administrator.

The Distinction Between Merit and Worth

The Duties-Based Approach focuses on teacher merit, but the merit of a teacher is not the only factor that must be taken into account in personnel decisions. There is also the worth of the teacher to the school or district. Being well known and liked in a district because one grew up there is likely to be valuable for school-community relations, although it has nothing to do with professional qualifications. Versatility in academic coverage is another value that transcends the performance of immediate duties; it lies in the area

---

[15]The resources available, not the ability available. The difference is crucial. If the ability isn't enough, that is no excuse; if the resources make it impossible to do the job, that is an excuse.

of potentiality. Teachers of Italian, however excellent, are of little worth to a school if demographic changes mean that there are no longer any students who wish to take that subject. This in no way reflects on their merit as teachers. Worth is a system notion; merit is a personal one. Worth is extrinsic and situational; merit is intrinsic and professional. Distinguishing between proper and improper uses of worth factors requires extensive discussion of particular examples.

The Basic Dimensions of Teacher Merit

The merit of a teacher can be exhaustively categorized in four ways:
- The quality of the content of teacher materials and student learning (including the love of learning).
- The quantity of student learning (including the extent of the love of learning).
- The professionalism with which the teacher's job is done (including all duties, not just teaching).
- The ethics with which the job is done.

Some have argued that these four categories can be reduced in two ways. First, it has been suggested that professionalism is simply a means to an end, and that end is covered in the first two dimensions. Someone who taught marvelous material with enormous success surely could not be downgraded for ignoring all the rules of the game. But the job of a teacher is not just teaching, and the professionalism dimension picks up all the rest. Also, the rules of the game in this case are not just advice about the best way to do things; they are requirements for how they should be done, so we have to include professionalism to ensure justice in the way classrooms are run. And finally, they are also likely to improve success. Since we are essentially never going to be able to pick up all the long-term learning that a teacher produces (the quality dimension), we have to settle for checking on short-term learning. But we can—and need to—buttress the bet that short-term learning is a good indicator of long-term learning by looking at whether the approach is professional (because a professional approach increases the chances of long-term effectiveness). For example, sound test construction and marking are more likely to pick up on places where further instruction is required and to do so in time to provide that instruction.

But aren't style indicators based on exactly the same claim of improved long-term effectiveness? It is crucial for those using the duties-based approach to understand fully the difference between using criteria of professionalism and using style indicators. Both are supposedly indicators of success. The difference lies simply in their status as obligations.

Professionalism is an obligation; that it also increases the chance of success is a bonus. Style is quite different. Since it is clear that many teachers of the highest quality—perhaps the best teachers—do not use the style that research has shown to be the most successful, one cannot argue that the obligatory way to teach is to follow the winning style. But the best way to test involves giving valid tests, in each and every case, because justice requires it and also because it leads to better diagnosis.

Ethical vs. Professional. A second suggestion for compressing the list of basic criteria is very different. It begins with the suggestion that ethics is simply part of professionalism. The point is sound in principle, but we normally distinguish between *codes of professional ethics,* which usually refer to matters specific to a profession (in teaching, we condemn taking bribes for giving high marks), and *recommended procedures* within a profession, such as using distracters in multiple-choice questions that are about equally attractive to a student who has not studied the material.

A deeper analysis links all four of the criteria into one—the notion of duty. It is the duty of the professional teacher to ensure that the quality requirement is met, that the quantity learned is as high as possible consistent with other duties, and that ethical standards are met. Hence the system set out here is monolithically based on the notion of professional duty, although that structure incorporates the four dimensions.

The Professional Duties of a Teacher

At this point, we must divide the notion of duty into a more specific set of obligations. This is the heart of the matter: it is a long list of the teacher's professional duties compiled on the basis of validity, not ease of measurement. It's a list that avoids any reference to style or any other indicators that cannot be shown to be necessary consequences of the duties of the job. In Figure 5.1, each category is described as a dimension, or sometimes as a criterion. The latter is based on the logical use of the term, according to which criteria definitely constitute an entity's essence, and the fact that these criteria (allegedly) define the teacher's job. (The distinction is between criteria and mere indicators which are only empirically linked with doing the job well. But "criterion" is sometimes used to refer to the standards that must be met on each dimension. To avoid confusion, therefore, "dimension" is used except when it is necessary to distinguish criteria from indicators.

The list in Figure 5.1 is based on sources that include a number of official documents that make some attempt at the same goal. A more important source has been the suggestions and reactions of several hundred experienced teachers and school administrators in Australia, the United States, and Canada. As we have proceeded through version after version, each new group was asked, "How would you, as a teacher, feel about being rated according to the way you perform the items on this list? What is missing that should be included, and what is included that should be omitted?"

Figure 5.1
The Teacher's Professional Duties

1. Knowledge of Duties
Includes knowledge of the law and regulations applying to schools in a district or a state as well as the expectations at a particular school (e.g., division of responsibility in team teaching situations; expectations of assistance with out-of-class activities such as syllabus design, materials selection, school projects, clubs and societies, special student review). Includes understanding of the curriculum requirements and the duties in the following list.

2. Knowledge of School and Community
Includes an understanding of any special characteristics, background, or ideology of the school, its staff and students, and of its environment. This is part of the *needs assessment* for planning lessons and curriculums (jobs available, languages spoken, family educational level) and of the *resources inventory* (parks, libraries, museums, tertiary institutions, factories) that should affect instructional planning. And it assists with determining what standards of teaching, and what expectations as to dress and conduct—in school and out—to adopt or protest. (Should homework be set? What grading standards are used?)

3. Knowledge of Subject Matter
A. In the field(s) of special competence
Subject matter knowledge should be at least enough to ensure that appropriate materials can be selected or prepared and explained, and that student understanding of them can be appropriately tested; and to ensure that most questions can be answered correctly. Where questions cannot be answered, it must be known where answers can be found quickly (this requirement of "resource awareness" includes museums, art galleries, etc., as well as reference works). Suggested guidelines for minimum subject matter competence are—for high school teachers—two years of successful tertiary study of each subject taught, and one year of such study for primary teachers. A degree with a major in the subject should be expected where teaching of college preparatory courses is involved. Competency tests to ensure the continued presence of the equivalent level of knowledge are an obligation of the employer (and often also of the training institution), since: (i) even for recent graduates, a certificate from a credentialing institution cannot be counted on to provide that assurance, and (ii) for mid-career teachers, some knowledge and skills have evaporated or become outdated, and (iii) other knowledge has been added to what is covered by that standard since they graduated, often representing a large part of the curriculum (earth studies) and sometimes representing most of it (computer studies).

B. In across-the-curriculum subjects like English, study skills, personal/vocational awareness, computer studies, etc.
While only a minimum level of competence is required, that includes a good tertiary level of literacy in writing, speaking, and editing (which, for example, excludes nearly all spelling, punctuation, and grammatical errors); a modest competence in the use of computers in the classroom; and similarly for the other areas. Some of these areas have been added to the obligations of teachers quite recently. With or without adequate inservice training, they become part of the obligations of the teacher. The task here is not to determine whether it is reasonable or unreasonable to include them, but only to determine what is now understood to be part of the obligations of a professional teacher.

4. Instructional Design
A. Course design
The teacher should be able to develop course plans from a knowledge of what is required by the local curriculum regulations and testing mileposts, together with information (which

Continued

Figure 5.1 (continued)

may have to be researched) about student ability/achievement levels, and available resources. Course plans typically include: a list of objectives or topics for lessons and terms (course outlines); activity, project, lab, library, homework, test, and field trip descriptions located on a timeline; at an appropriate level for each class; and in a form adequate for use by a replacement teacher or supervisor. Versions of these may be provided to the class, if this is helpful rather than inhibitive of note taking or inquiry skill development. Note that no requirement is included for detailed lesson plan (behavioral objectives, activities in ten-minute segments, etc.), although these are sometimes a useful device, especially for beginning teachers.

B. Selection and creation of materials
(Applies to the extent that the teacher is allowed/required to select or add materials to those provided.) Teaching materials, selected or created to fit into the instruction plan, should be current, correct, comprehensive, and—where possible—well designed. They should, where possible, provide or include references, applications, and enrichment resources as well as basic instructional assistance (unless this is covered by the text or other materials); where possible they should incorporate a variety of instructional and doctrinal approaches, for the benefit of students who respond better to an approach other than that provided by the teacher; alternative viewpoints should be presented fairly, so that students can consider the range of views; and there should be enough to supplement presentations by the instructor, visitors, trips, texts, etc.

C. Competent use of material resources
Appropriate use of materials, library, computers, field trips, laboratory and specialist personnel (e.g., librarian, school psychologist). This use must demonstrate "informed use" competencies. At the simplest level, chalkboard writing and overhead transparencies, and the writing and diagrams in paper handouts must be readable, a test which many tertiary teachers would fail. (It is helpful to have explicit or implicit knowledge of the simple guidelines on number of words per line and lines per overhead that guarantee legibility in the average classroom.) Preferably, the teacher should be able to use those more complex audiovisual and computer technologies for which significant resources are available in the relevant teaching area. Systematic and objective evaluations of available materials by self or others should be used as the basis for selection. There is no absolute need to use media or specialists in order to do good teaching; but if they are available, and will significantly improve teaching the particular subject to these particular students, at a cost which is well below the benefits, the professional should be able to use them.

D. Course and curriculum evaluation
The teacher (in, and out of, class) should be able to employ discussion, individual interviews, observations, questionnaires, and testing—formal or informal—to gather and systematically record data for later analysis in order to get: (i) needs and ability assessments with respect to content, level, approach, and pacing; (ii) information about the success of curriculum options and instruction. (These goals do not require individual test results, the need for which is covered below.)

E. Needs of special groups
Knowledge of the needs of special groups that may be encountered is important, including the hearing- and sight-impaired, blacks and Asians, nonnative speakers, fast and slow learners.

F. Use of human resources
The preceding efforts should be supplemented by involving specialist personnel (curriculum specialists, audiovisual and methods specialists) where appropriate.

5. Gathering Information About Student Learning

A. Testing skills

As a basis for advice on student progress, to students and their advisers (and administrative authorities), the teacher must create or select, and administer, suitable tests (construed in the widest sense to include structured observation, project analysis, etc.). Tests should: match the content or skills covered in the teaching and required curriculum (including assigned out-of-class work) at the difficulty level appropriate for the class; be unambiguous; not be overcued; have one and only one correct answer when only one answer is allowed as correct; be answerable by a typical student who did the classwork and homework but not by just any student; indicate the marks or relative importance of each question; relate to useful continuing and future competencies, in an interesting way where possible; allow the student to display creativity, understanding, and the capacity to synthesize and evaluate—where possible and appropriate; be specific enough to provide evidence to guide counseling and modification of class materials where appropriate. To do this requires a minimum level of professional understanding of the advantages and disadvantages of testing in general and of various types of tests, including: multiple-choice, short and long answer, verbal and written, structured observation, interview, and project tests. The teacher should understand the difference between and be able to construct appropriate tests for summative, formative, and diagnostic purposes; the difference between tests for ranking and for grading, and between norm-referenced and criterion-referenced tests; and should understand the use of matrix-sampling and item analysis. If multiple-choice tests are used, it must be understood how to construct them so as to measure higher-level cognitive skills (a feasible but rather difficult task). The construction of rating forms for feedback by students on teaching and teacher materials should also be well understood.

B. Grading knowledge (marking, scoring, rating, diagnosing)

Should understand the difference between: holistic and analytic scoring and the advantages of each; the design and use of scoring keys ("rubrics"); the fallacy of the "A for effort" approach; typical sizes of test-retest and interjudge differences; magnitude of test-anxiety effect; how to recognize serious learning disabilities, etc.

C. Grading process

To the extent possible, this must be done to avoid bias, especially on essay-type questions, by: using coded papers; marking question by question, rather than paper by paper; changing the order in which papers are marked from question to question; remarking early papers to pick up any drift of standards; using and improving a scoring key. The reasons for each of these procedures should be understood.

D. Grade allocation

Grades should be awarded *consistently* (equal grades for equal quality/quantity of work); *appropriately* (no B's or A's for work that is merely satisfactory for students at that level, no F's for work that is around the satisfactory level, etc.); and *helpfully* (on standards that relate to the needs of the students; on parts or aspects of work as well as on whole performance, when the test materials are being returned).

6. Providing Information About Student Learning

A. To each student.

(i) On class performance. The teacher should provide—in class or, when more appropriate, in writing or in private discussion—an indication of how the instructor thinks the student relates in quality/quantity of response (if the latter is required) to the standards expected and preferably also to the range of quality of peer responses, especially if there is any chance of misunderstanding by a student of his or her comparative or absolute level of performance.

Continued

Figure 5.1 (continued)

(ii) On each test. The teacher gives correct answers, explains the grading/marking standards, and the individual grades when necessary, comments on common errors, preferably distributes examples of fully worked good and bad answers with comments (not necessarily using real answers, or ones from the same class).

B. To the administration
In the typical school context, the teacher must provide the administration with information about student performance on a regular and timely basis as required; must identify problem behavior, and facility or support deficiencies; must call for assistance as necessary.

C. To parents, guardians, and other appropriate authorities
The teacher communicates to those with a right to know, and only to them, as to how the individual students or classes are progressing. Preferably, has the skills to enlist support from these people in the enterprise of motivating and assisting the students in learning.

7. Classroom Skills
A. Communication skills
The teacher must be able to communicate information, explanations, justifications, expectations, directions, and evaluations to students of the age and abilities that will be encountered in the place of employment. Success in communication requires efficiency and clarity in presentation and skill in the maintenance of attention. Competence in the engendering of motivation is desirable. Similar communication skills are required with respect to peers and parents, supervisors, and sometimes community groups. Complete determination of this competence would depend on later outcome checks, but something can be picked up in the course of a classroom visit by a specially trained observer. (There remain the difficulties that the sample observed is not random, is too small, is usually judgmentally assessed, and only refers to short-term success.)

B. Management skills
(i) Under emergency conditions. Teachers have moral as well as legal responsibility for coping to the extent possible with what happens in an emergency. In particular, they should know what to do in case any of the following is possible in their area: (i) fire; (ii) flood; (iii) tornado/typhoon; (iv) earthquake; (v) volcanic eruption; (vi) civil disorder (riots, tear gas, bombs, mob's or strikers' entry to classroom); (viii) trauma, notably fractures, snakebite (or spider/scorpion bite), stab or gunshot wounds, electrocution, choking, gas poisoning, and seizures. (Five of the eight have occurred within the last decade in each of a number of metropolitan areas.) Field trips or overnight stays introduce other hazards such as the risk of drowning, which engenders the duty of mastering CPR techniques and the identification of poisonous plants, snakes, spiders, etc.

(ii) Under standard conditions. Teachers must have the ability to control classroom behavior so that learning is readily possible—and can be assisted—for all students at all times, while preserving principles of justice and avoiding excessively repressive conditions. Justice requires making clear what the rules and penalties for breaking them are, and enforcing them consistently. It should include the ability to cope with a range of useful class modes including whole-class and small-group discussions, questioning, question-answering, and listening; it is desirable though possibly not essential to have the ability to achieve high time-on-task ratio; certainly it is important to have the skills to deal with student inquiries in such a way as to encourage the inquirer to further exploration. Lack of classroom control leads to disruption of the school and not just the classroom, either through direct (noise) impact or through the grapevine; and it leads to severe penalties for the students who are willing but unable to learn because it is occurring in or near their classroom. So it is rightly considered a minimum necessary condition for competence. But a quiet classroom is not

necessarily a learning classroom, and evaluation systems that just reward silence are seriously flawed.

8. Personal Characteristics

A. *Professional attitude.* The teacher should be able to accept criticism constructively unless the criticism is demonstrably invalid or redundant; should solicit critical evaluation of various aspects of job performance from time to time, including student evaluations where possible; should exhibit a positive attitude toward students and to teaching as a vocation; be helpful to parents, peers, and administration with respect to legitimate requests; be helpful to apprentice or paraprofessional teachers; must not evidence prejudices related to race, religion, age, gender, etc.; must be punctual and conscientious in performance of duties; must be compassionate as well as just in dealing with students; must, in general, be highly ethical in dealing with all job responsibilities and personnel; must try to avoid penalizing students in the course of industrial or personal disputes. Standards of language and deportment must be consistent with knowledge of possible impact on students.

Note (i): Being noticeably "under the influence" of drugs such as alcohol while on duty is thus prima facie evidence of serious misconduct since it will affect capacity to perform the primary tasks, and probably affect respect for the individual and the staff in general, with consequent long-term costs in student learning. But being under the influence in the pub on Saturday night is part of the right to enjoy oneself in one's own way, as long as it doesn't interfere with the rights of others.

Note (ii): Leadership skills or achievements, often included as desirable for teachers, are completely inappropriate entries; they make a good basis for selecting future administrators, which is why they get mentioned, but they are entirely unnecessary for good teaching. The same applies to "good at working in groups" unless it is a duty of the position that team-teaching be done. Some committee work is no doubt a common obligation, and should be rated on outcomes, not presumed components.

Note (iii): Counseling or "pastoral care" skills would be appropriate for some jobs and not for others; the job description should be clear on this point.

Note (iv): There is a legal "duty of care" meaning the duty to take care of students who are in your charge (especially when they are too young to do so without your help). Beyond this, it is arguable that a teacher should "care about them." But there is no duty to care for them *as if they were your own*, or even *as if you liked them all*. This is an area where well-meaning administrators often require more than is appropriate. It is crucial to professional service that "distancing" be possible, or else the stress load becomes intolerable for many teachers we can ill afford to lose. The commitment declines with the age of the student, so that at the primary and secondary (though not the tertiary level) it is important that teachers have a real concern for children's welfare, including their self-esteem. (This does not, however, entail a heavy-handed positive reinforcement strategy in primary school.)

Note (v): Enthusiasm for the subject matter cannot be justified as a requirement. A "positive attitude" toward teaching, recommended above, is fully compatible with radical and sustained specific criticism of its condition and management. It is incompatible with unremitting and unconstructive denigration, which has a very serious effect on others, especially beginners.

B. *Professional development*
Teachers should have good awareness of their own areas of strength and weakness and implement systematic procedures for self-evaluation and development where appropriate. This might include evaluation of their time- and stress-management ability; engaging in

Continued

Figure 5.1 (continued)

systematic improvement of class materials and plans; experimenting with variations of method and/or materials to produce steady improvement; soliciting input from students and peers; engaging in systematic reading or other study of current developments in pedagogy and educational/text materials in the teacher's area of specialization; being able to set out the results of the preceding efforts in a professional portfolio.

9. Service to the Profession
A. Knowledge about professional issues
Without some knowledge about the profession (its nature, role, history, current problems and issues), there can be little effective service to it. Without service to it, there is little of the profession about it.

B. Professional ethics
Knowledge about (and performance in accordance with) the standards of the profession, e.g., in not representing oneself as presenting the school's viewpoint unless specifically empowered to do so. Providing a good role model for peers and trainees; perhaps assisting with activities such as the development and enforcement of professional ethical standards.

C. Helping beginners and peers
Providing systematic assistance to beginners and student teachers should be regarded as part of the essential commitment to professionalism.

D. Work on projects for other professionals
Examples include working on a newsletter or journal, organizing a study group or making seminar arrangements, or working for a union. These would be appropriate though not mandatory.

On this point, many of the official documents we now see are quite inadequate. They rarely include more than two-thirds of the items on the list, and they nearly always include a number of items that are not duties at all, or not duties in most school jurisdictions. The better documents we see now often derive from an earlier edition of this list, which has been widely circulated. (This may suggest that it's time for some more external criticism.) The order used here is not a presumed order of importance, but an approximation of the order of dependence. That is, the earlier items are usually required before the latter ones can be fully handled by the evaluator.

Standards and Definitions

It would be unreasonable to expect a very high level of performance on every one of the dimensions, but none can be entirely dismissed. A minimum level of achievement on every one is required, and a substantial level of achievement on most is expected. Less would be accepted if the reasons for the exceptions were good and only rarely invoked. Exactly what this means varies in particular circumstances, and some case studies that illustrate limits must be included in any training workshops. It is clear that merely adding up the score across all duties is an invalid integrative procedure. The minimums must be achieved on each, and a failure to meet them can't be traded off against over-minimum scores elsewhere. If the minimums are not met, totaling depends on weighting the dimensions. It is never easy to justify differential weight, but one might argue for halving the weights of items 1, 2, and 9.

There is no doubt room for improvement of the list. However, improvements will probably be in the nature of refinements rather than radical alternatives because the term "teacher" is generally understood to include these duties. It is highly unlikely that any user of the English language would contend that classroom teachers should not have the duties listed in Figure 5.1; certainly items 3-7 and probably item 8 are part of the everyday concept. The details of these and the other items consistently emerge as part of what experienced teachers and school administrators feel are duties of the profession.

Thus, we have a response to the question people often naively think must be answered before any study of the evaluation of teaching can be done: How do you define good teaching? The real situation is that one works toward that definition through continuing study of the field. It is a major goal of serious research, not a minor preliminary to it. Good teaching is whatever scores well on the duties list, with the provisos just mentioned (and some aspects detailed in the next few sections).

The test of whether a given factor is part of the definition of "good teaching" must be distinguished from the question of whether teachers at a particular moment in history think it is a preferred practice. Preferred practices are bets about what works in achieving whatever the definition of good teaching requires. They are not part of the meaning of the term. Yet we often find studies where the distinction just made is confused, and it is suggested that practices which are excellent in some areas and irrelevant to other areas are part of the very meaning of good teaching (i.e., highly organized presentations). Socrates would have failed on this criterion, which is a counter-example to the view that it's part of the definition. Organization, like eloquent speech and evident enthusiasm for the subject matter, are style variables. A skilled helper can recommend them, with care and some risk, and there are reasons to consider doing so in some cases. But a competent judge cannot use those standards. The formative context is critically different from the summative.

Rules of Evidence

Instead of going into step-by-step details on documentation, which would be extremely lengthy, what follows are some general comments about evaluating teacher performance on each dimension in Figure 5.1. (Note that the suggestions are validity oriented, not politics oriented. The earlier comment about political compromises applies here.)

In general, more than one source of evidence—and preferably more than two—should be used to document performance on each criterion. These matters are all prone to some inaccuracy, many of them prone to understandable bias, and their importance demands confirmation. Where possible, the sources should be independent (not subject to effects from the other sources).

It is essential that in all cases the teacher—like the reviewers—has the opportunity to see and respond to all evidence. This immediately provides a second source of data on most dimensions, though not a fully independent one. (The exception is where overwhelming considerations of confidentiality apply.)

Whenever estimates from various sources substantially differ, further investigation must be undertaken if there is any chance that it will resolve the issue.

In no case is automatic averaging of estimates justified. The person in charge of personnel decisions is responsible for making decisions about which sources of data or judgment to take into account at all and what weights to assign to testimony or dimensions.[16] (There will of course be some individual judgments or dimensions in some individual cases where averaging is the best policy, but the evaluator should make and be responsible for that decision.) In turn, the principal component in the evaluation of the evaluator is the care and skill with which the evaluation of teachers is performed.

Significant and systematic inaccuracy by any estimator,[17] revealed by comparing that person's ratings with objective data or with others' ratings, is sometimes a sign of professional incompetence and should be rated as such. For example, a teacher who constantly overrates his or her own performance is showing poor self-evaluation, a required skill for any professional. To an even greater extent, since this skill represents a larger proportion of the relevant professional repertoire, the personnel evaluator is vulnerable to criticism for biased or inaccurate ratings, and any evidence of this should automatically be entered into his or her files.

Systematic inaccuracy should also be used as a basis for extrapolating with a correction factor to ensure that no one suffers or benefits from persistent bias.

It is important that teachers collect as much documentation relating to their discharge of duties as possible. This reduces reliance on judgment or

---

[16]Weights only come in for rewards, since no weighting can, in general, offset a failure to achieve minimum standards. Deviations from unitary weighting are always very hard to justify, but should be determined in advance and announced to applicants.

[17]The estimators are the subevaluators, those whose ratings are being combined by the evaluator to achieve the overall evaluation.

memory. This "teacher portfolio," for which teachers are entirely responsible, [18] should be part of their official personnel file, considered whenever reviews occur. Work on it should be supported by appropriate inservice workshops. Providing such documentation should be considered part of the professional skill repertoire, partly because it is relevant to good self-evaluation and partly because it is a contribution to the effective governance of schools.

An appeal process for all parties is essential. It need not be an exhaustive process, and almost all appeals should be managed by an arbitrator whose secondary commitment is to develop a set of guiding principles and case law that will reduce the necessity for large numbers of appeals. Appeals should not be heard unless they raise a serious question. Appealing without appropriate grounds is itself, in some case, unprofessional conduct.

Evaluation systems like the one proposed here are complex and should never be attempted as one-shot implementations. Stage I should be a one-year test for volunteers only, under a no-harm guarantee, and should lead to significant refinements. Stage II should be a two- or three-year trial with serious external examination.

If the school principal is to be the main evaluator, his or her duties must be redefined so that staff evaluation and development occupy the top 25 percent of the workstack; that is, nothing short of safety emergencies should preempt this commitment. This responsibility should probably be worth 50 percent of the points in the evaluation of the administrator (because the worth to the district is so high.)

Sources of Evidence

Evidence refers, at least, to the following: expert testimony *in the area of demonstrable expertise*, "found data" (existing records), incidental or specially arranged observations, and the results of tests and experiments. The way to set up a systematic approach is with a matrix that shows how each duty will be covered by data from two or three of the following sources. Exactly how that matrix looks depends on the local situation. (Are there assistant principals? What does the contract allow? How many teachers have to be reviewed?)

● *Judgments*—by the teacher being evaluated, other teachers, department heads, counselors, students, parents, principals, district personnel, inservice providers. [19]

---

[18]Apart from annotations from reviewers, which have been seen by the teacher, and to which the teacher's responses may be appended.

[19]Of course, there is no suggestion that, for example, fellow teachers be asked for an across-the-board evaluation of the teacher. They are not in any position to give any such evaluation. On the other hand, teachers with expertise in the same subjects would be good judges of materials and grading standards.

- *Found data*—school records, applications for the teacher's classes, attendance, grade distribution, recommended texts, student work, tests, class handouts, assignments. Teacher records include lesson plans and a log of notes on students, classes, or success of materials. Personnel records include the original job description, letters of support and complaint, applications for transfer, enrollment and grade records, library records (assignments and checkouts).

- *Observations*—in the classroom (constrained to duties only), on the school grounds, in the teachers room, in committee meetings, in dealing with parents/peers/students/counselors. Includes observations by students, peers, and administrators.

- *Test data*—relating to students of this teacher or classes in which the teacher participated and including comparative performance, absolute performance, success of particular approaches, materials, or teams. Testing may be done by others (i.e., state competency tests).

- *Teacher portfolio*—self-evaluation and personal development plan, results of experiments and reading program. Courses taken, procedures used in grading, basis for selection of materials.

- *Footprint data*—the results of exit interviews with graduating seniors are often valuable additions to the data. Other data include college applications and acceptances, scholarships, and changes in the curriculum due to the teacher's committee work.

Advantages of the Duties-Based Approach

Perhaps the most important advantage of the duties-based approach (DBTE) is that it avoids the use of illicit material and inappropriate judges, thereby reducing the chances of injustice and large legal damages. In particular, it places strict limits on what can be picked up from classroom observation. Also, it brings in a good many important factors that are normally overlooked in evaluation, from the quality of content to performance on committees. This feature of DBTE means that it gives a better picture of the teacher's total contribution, including the out-of-classroom contribution, and makes the teacher feel that these dimensions of performance are appreciated. Third, DBTE brings in sources of evidence that are often ignored, most notably the teacher portfolio and the student ratings, but also the footprint data, which increase the weight given to long-term student benefits. And there is an overall improvement in the solidity of the evidence and in the sense of participation on the part of the teacher and the students, whose input is so important (though this is a judgment based only on anecdotal evidence). Fourth, DBTE encourages rigid segregation of formative from summative evaluation, to improve the rights of teachers to be judged for what they do, not judged on whose instructions they follow. This segregation also improves the chances that the support system will be utilized.

The Teacher Development System

Now that I have explained the Duties-Based approach to summative evaluation, I will elaborate on the development system that should accompany it.

The general thrust of inservice should be driven by the results of staff evaluations. It seems clear, for example, that one of the most serious deficiencies in teacher preparation and practice is in test-construction skills. This is highly teachable and might be built into a series of inservice sessions required of those who do not pass a pretest. (And it should probably be joined by computer skills for the substantial number of teachers who have not yet acquired them.)

One might suppose that this, at last, is the area where one can use all the research on the relative effectiveness of different approaches. Unfortunately, the matter is not that simple. The research does have a place here, but it has to be very carefully circumscribed. Even in preservice training, it can only be used within strict limits.

It's best to distinguish two kinds of situations from which the teacher comes to inservice. In the standard updating inservices, demonstrations of and workshops on research-based approaches are desirable as long as they are not required of all staff members. What improves one teacher may damage another. We know from the statistics in the better studies on direct instruction, for example, that teachers tend to improve their performance, measured rather simplistically, on material that suits their approach, at least for students in certain age ranges. What we don't know is how many teachers of material quite different from that on which the direct instruction approach has been validated would have their performance damaged by adopting this approach (i.e., teachers of moral education or literature or current affairs). In fact, because there are no comprehensive studies, we don't even know whether the ones that show the short-term gain deteriorate below their initial performance in the long run. If inservice attendance is compulsory, you must offer more than one parallel activity. And if one of the options is a workshop on method, make sure the alternative to it has nothing to do with method.

The second type of situation—the last-chance scenario—calls for more desperate measures. In this case, a teacher has been identified as unsatisfactory and must show improvement (not the same as "must attend specified remedial exercises and do the required assignments") or else lose the job or status. In a last chance situation, the helper should indeed recommend to the teacher—remember, it's still the teacher's option as a professional to accept or reject advice on remediation—the best research-based approach available.

Two things are known that were not known in the regular updating situation. It is known that this teacher's natural style doesn't work, and it is known that the risk of having his or her teaching modified for the worse is not the most serious risk. And direct instruction is probably the best bet around, at least for applications similar to those for which it has been validated and for teachers whose alternatives are known to be unsatisfactory.

Mentors

A key aspect of the teacher development system is the availability of support staff who can assist teachers in their improvement efforts. Various people can serve in these helper roles. One important possibility that also addresses the need to extend the upper level of the salary scale for good teachers is the mentor position. In fact, the mentor position is almost an essential creation if a district is to show that it really does value teaching.

Instead of the usual arrangement where the best salaries in the district go only to administrators, the mentor is selected simply on teaching merit and is paid a salary that runs up through that of principals of smaller schools. There are only a few mentors in a district (ideally about 1 to every 50-100 teachers), so that the job is prestigious and not too expensive. The appointment, although renewable, has to be re-earned in open competition every three years. It is an award—a salary increase against increased expectations in the future—not a reward, something given in recognition of past performance. It would make a travesty of the position to assume that superior teaching skills—any more than competent teaching skills—do not deteriorate, since one would soon have mentors who had burned out or stopped keeping their teaching up to date once they got the award. The only requirement of the position is to give other teachers (including student teachers) visiting privileges—one at a time—to the mentor's classroom. Also, the mentor must be willing to talk about teaching informally and occasionally with other teachers at the same school.

An option of the job is to do some formal helping of teachers who request it—up to 40 percent of time, if that can be accommodated by the timetable and the district's funding. It can't be made a requirement of the job, or your new way to reward good teachers requires that they take on teacher-training work instead of administration. Similarly, professed willingness to undertake the larger role cannot be taken into account in selecting mentors or reappointing them. The mentor must be seen as primarily a super-teacher whose benefits are primarily to the students. They can only guarantee that they will be role models not that they will be good teachers of teachers. We know that the best swimming coaches sometimes can't swim at all, let alone well, and that the best football players are often hopeless as coaches. We should not build the mentor system on the opposite assumption.

Mentor help may be made available to staff members from nearby schools, if the need at the mentor's own school is met first and the mentor, principals, and district approve.

It is unlikely—and not essential—that the school system will offer extra released time to the teachers who take advantage of the help. This time can be covered under regular inservice time or as an after-hours activity.

The helping option is compensated for with released time for the mentor, and performance as a helper is largely evaluated by those who use it, though it may be monitored for accountability purposes.

If the mentor exercises the formal helping option, then a confidentiality requirement applies. It would be ideal if no information about the occurrence, extent, or results of helping interactions is passed on by the mentor to anyone else. But accountability must apply to the mentor as well as to teachers, and it makes a complete ban impossible. Hence, the names of those getting assistance—which might, of course, be assistance in going from good to excellent—must be provided to the principal, along with an indication of the time spent with each, so that the principal can give and collect from these individuals their rating of the mentor. What cannot be passed on is any suggestion as to the mentor's view of their merit or their diligence. A hearing for instant loss of mentor ranking, and loss of job, follows upon a breach of that condition.

Mentors should probably have someone in the district, or at least the state office, to whom they can turn for assistance with their helping roles (for example, to get copies of materials).

Mentors should normally be associated with schools rather than free-floating, though a mix of the two is possible. Otherwise, they are likely to exercise seniority rights to congregate in the most-favored school in the district, abandoning the schools with the most needs. Teachers at a school, and any willing to transfer to it, must both be eligible to apply. It is desirable not to give preference to those from the school, since their better knowledge of local conditions is offset by their lack of independence and lack of familiarity with alternative approaches. This avoids "closed-shop" expectations growing up into a norm that makes it difficult to bring in new blood. A mentor should be appointed when a teaching vacancy occurs and the principal or teachers as well as the district feel that it would be desirable to have a mentor at that site.

Conclusion

We have reviewed a number of feasible approaches to teacher evaluation. It seems clear that only one is valid, but it is relatively untried. What should the sensible school administrator do at this point? What should teachers support and encourage?

It's a good general principle in educational administration to let others play guinea pig. Moving only to the tried and true avoids wasting effort on debugging new approaches. Quite often the fashion proves a flash in the pan so that the need to change evaporates.

The situation is different here. Although we cannot point to long track records with the proposed system as a totality, there is nothing unfamiliar about its data sources or the duties to which it appeals for validity. In fact, we have good evidence that the administrative infrastructure for this kind of approach is perfectly workable. And the alternative is to continue using a system that is demonstrably unjust and almost certain to incur expensive penalties.

When you discover an uncontrollable fire in the classroom, you cannot hesitate to take the students to a new building on the grounds that it lacks a long occupancy record.

From the teacher's point of view, it is surely preferable to work with an appraisal system that fully recognizes the great range of a teacher's duties and does not change with every new batch of research results. The appropriate response is surely to eliminate from existing practice as quickly as possible every use of style criteria or impressionistic judgment, replacing them with duty-related data.

Brady L. Gadberry, Jr.

From the Practitioner's Point of View...

Scriven makes a strong case that present methods of teacher evaluation are fatally flawed by the inclusion of invalid elements. Contending that present methods are "arbitrary," "unjust," "intrusive," "invalid," or "unable to provide adequate information," he proposes what he considers a valid alternative. Although his arguments are compelling, I believe that under close scrutiny Scriven's plan is also defective.

It is not possible, in a short critique, to give this plan the detailed analysis it deserves. Nonetheless, certain areas must be addressed. For instance, Scriven makes a great effort to convince us that any evaluation based on teaching style is not only invalid, but also violates natural justice. He uses a generalization about areas of discrimination to make his case for invalidating the use of generalization in evaluating teaching styles.

Generalizations can be helpful if not misused. If we taste 50 green apples and all are sour, we can make a valid generalization that green apples tend to be sour and a reasonably sound prediction that green apple number 51 will also probably be sour; it's not a certainty, but it is a high probability. Similar generalizations can be made about teaching style. Even the courts will allow such conclusions in civil cases because they function on the premise that decisions are based on a preponderance of the evidence.

Scriven states, ". . . it is essentially certain that generalizations will always be falsified, so it is essentially certain that those who use them will make mistakes and hence commit injustices and waste resources." He thus provides an example of a dreadfully misused generalization. In an ironic sense it does support Scriven's position, but for the wrong reasons. He has done what he is trying to prevent others from doing.

Teaching style is important and generalizations about style can be helpful in evaluation; however, using any generalization requires extreme caution, as Scriven has shown.

The other elements he describes are also invalidated by logic more than by examples of what actually has happened in the classroom. I would caution anyone about accepting Scriven's logic without carefully analyzing specific, actual classroom events.

If we accept Scriven's premise that existing systems of evaluation are flawed and invalid, then we must judge his alternative plan with a critical eye to see how it avoids those same flaws.

Brady L. Gadberry, Jr., is Principal of Henderson Junior High School in Little Rock, Arkansas, where he has served for the past 18 years. During his career he has represented both the teachers' union and the administration in the development of teacher evaluation procedures.

From a practical viewpoint, Scriven's plan is not an evaluation plan; it is a list of the professional duties of a teacher. The list is excellent, but not exhaustive; other criteria and indicators could be added. Scriven also states that the list is based on validity, not ease of measurement. Indeed, some of the dimensions, such as personal characteristics, are practically impossible to measure.

From a logistical viewpoint, there is nothing in the Scriven plan to indicate that it would work. He establishes "standards"—dimensions of teacher merit—but he leaves the level of performance expectations nebulous. Nothing in the plan is tied together. There is no model.

Scriven has gone to great lengths to show that there are many problems in teacher evaluation. While some of his logic needs further examination, it would be difficult to argue with his conclusion that our current systems are badly, perhaps even fatally, flawed. He also presents, with his alternative plan, a good description of the job of a professional teacher. However, what Scriven calls a valid alternative is not a plan; it is a concept. And that concept seems also to be flawed because it probably cannot be made into a workable model that could be used by a school system. Regardless of the intent, the validity of the elements, or the logic of the author, a concept is of little value in teacher evaluation unless it can be developed into a usable model.

6 Evaluation of Teaching: The Cognitive Development View

ARTHUR L. COSTA, ROBERT J. GARMSTON,
LINDA LAMBERT

We have become convinced that the overt, visible skills (of teaching) are
driven by mental activities that constitute the invisible skills of teaching.
Joyce and Showers (1988)

Dear Superintendent Jergens:
Our deepest regrets at the trauma that you, the Board, Mrs. Halverson,
and certainly the children and parents have suffered in this situation. We
have some information currently of great use to some districts; whether it is
appropriate to your district will depend on several factors, including your
willingness and capacity to design this system with the local teachers'
association, your views of teaching, and several other important
considerations. To find out if this is for you, read on.
Art, Bob, and Linda

Arthur L. Costa is Professor of Education, California State University, Sacramento,
and 1988-89 President of the Association for Supervision and Curriculum Development. Robert J. Garmston is Professor of Education, California State University,
Sacramento. Linda Lambert is Associate Professor of Education, California State
University, Hayward.

It has been said that mankind is in search of three elusive goals: the Fountain of Youth, the Holy Grail, and the perfect evaluation system (Ludwig and Raddeau 1987). We do not offer you the perfect evaluation system, for we do not believe that one exists. We do offer an alternative perspective on teacher evaluation that is so bold, yet so sensible, that we are persuaded it will significantly improve the way professionals in your district go about the daily work of educating children. We propose an approach to evaluating "the invisible skills of teaching."

Evaluate that which is invisible? Yes, indeed, for those invisible skills are the thinking processes of teaching that manifest themselves in the work of educators. In this chapter, we present a compelling rationale for attending to teacher thinking in teacher evaluation programs. In the process, you will encounter a few "three-dollar words." We alert you to our intention to promote a new vocabulary along with a new perspective—and invite you to embark upon this journey with us fully prepared for some intriguing puzzlements, some rigorous frustrations, and some revolutionary insights.

Before we define a cognitive development view of evaluation, we will establish a context for our recommendations by addressing four central questions to any evaluation system.

1. Evaluation for what purpose?

2. What is the relationship of the area being evaluated to the work performed by teachers?

3. Is the evaluation system congruent with the district's view of teacher work?

4. To what degree can an evaluation system match conditions necessary for the successful operation of a teacher evaluation system?

Evaluation for What Purpose?

Within the last decade, there has been increasing attention to evaluating teachers' work. According to Darling-Hammond et al. (1983), much of this public attention comes from the perception that the key to educational improvement lies in upgrading the quality of teachers. States have responded with competency tests for teacher certification, licensure procedures, and legislative requirements for teacher evaluation. In the fall of 1987, the National Professional Standards Board was established under the auspices of the Carnegie Foundation. The intent behind these legislative actions has been to attract and retain excellent teachers and to facilitate the exodus of those who are not considered excellent.

As you reexamine your district's evaluation processes, it is important that you are clear about the purpose of evaluation. While some purposes are not mutually exclusive, an emphasis on one purpose may limit a district's ability to pursue another (Darling-Hammond et al. 1983). Some purposes are inconsistent with others. For example, gathering formative data to identify a supervision approach may be inconsistent with using those data for teacher dismissal. In supervision, the teacher must function as a "willing partner" (Costa and Garmston 1985, Glickman 1985, Sergiovanni and Corbally 1986); in dismissal, volition is replaced by the authority of the district. We are convinced that an evaluation system dominated by the need to weed out poor performers will itself perform poorly. Clear guidelines and agreements are needed so that inconsistencies do not undermine trust and, therefore, the capability for the district to function as a learning environment.

We propose (Figure 6.1) that districts consider four distinct purposes that may be served by teacher evaluation. Two focus on the teacher: improving teacher performance and informing personnel decisions about teachers. Two focus on the district: improving organizational performance and informing organizational decisions.

What Is the Relationship Between the Area Being Evaluated to the Work Being Performed?

Teachers perform many kinds of work. Here we are most concerned with the work that directly affects student performance. An increasing array of researchers report the essential nature that teacher decision-making has in selecting instructional behaviors that positively affect student learning (Berliner, Costa, and Garmston; Eisner, Hunter, Joyce, and Showers; Saphin; Shevelson; and Shulman). Teaching *is* thinking.

If teacher thinking improves, will teaching performance and student achievement improve? Research indicates that it will. Sprinthall and Theis-Sprinthall (1983) report compelling evidence that teachers who function at higher cognitive levels produce higher achievement in students. Characteristic of teachers at these higher levels is the ability to empathize, to symbolize experience, and to act in accordance with a disciplined commitment to human values. These teachers choose new practices when classroom problems occur, vary their use of instructional strategies, elicit more conceptual responses from students (Hunt and Joyce 1967), give more corrective and positive feedback to students (Calhoon 1985), and produce higher achieving students who are more cooperative and involved in their work (Harvey 1967). Witherall and Erickson (1978) found that teachers at the highest levels of ego development demonstrated greater complexity and commitment to the individual student, greater generation and use of data in teaching, and greater understanding of practices relating to rules, authority, and moral development. Glickman (1985) concluded that successful teachers are thoughtful teachers and they stimulate their students to be thoughtful as well.

Figure 6.1
Four Purposes of Teacher Evaluation

	Individual	Organization
	IMPROVE TEACHER PERFORMANCE	**IMPROVE ORGANIZATIONAL PERFORMANCE**
G A T H E R I N G **D A T A**	• Develop formative information about teaching performance. • Assess hiring criteria and job specifications. • Develop formative information about teacher characteristics and capacities. • Identify supervision goals. • Identify supervision approaches. • Model decision-making processes.	• Gather data about the effectiveness of the staff development system. • Gather data about the congruence between hypothetical and actual curriculum. • Measure student access to range and variety of teaching methodologies. • Identify organizational goals and action plans. • Assess school climate/trust level.
M A K I N G **D E C I S I O N S**	**INFORM PERSONNEL DECISIONS** • Produce summative information related to evaluation criteria. • Grant tenure. • Award promotions, advancements to leadership roles. • Administer disciplinary actions. • Dismiss teachers.	**INFORM ORGANIZATIONAL DECISIONS** • Design staff development program for subjects of teachers and administrators. • Initiate systemwide changes in expectations for instructional methodology. • Allocate budget resources for staff development, supervision, evaluation. • Align curriculum.

Of the 20 subfunctions of a comprehensive evaluation system, only one is for the sole purpose of dismissing teachers. However, many districts may be tempted to allow that motive to overwhelm other design considerations.

Is the Evaluation System Congruent with the District's View of Teachers' Work?

A teacher evaluation system must be congruent with a district's conception of teaching. Different conceptions imply different ways by which information is collected and judgments are made about teachers' work; and differing views reinforce teachers' perceptions about their own work. Teachers have been compared to craftpersons, bureaucrats, managers, laborers, and artists. We view teachers as skilled, autonomous, professional decision makers.

To sharpen the distinction of the teacher-as-professional from other views, let us consider teacher-as-laborer. Within the laborer conception, teaching activities are planned, organized, and routinized in the form of standard operating procedures. Teachers implement the prescribed instructional program and adhere to specified routines and procedures. The evaluation system involves inspecting the teacher's work and monitoring lesson plans and performance results. The school administrator is seen as a teacher's supervisor in the same way that a plant manager supervises a technician in a lab. This view of teaching assumes that effective practices can be predetermined and specified in concrete ways and that consistent adherence to these practices will produce the desired student outcomes.

When the teacher is viewed as a professional, however, teaching is seen as requiring a repertoire of specialized approaches and the exercise of judgment about when those approaches will be used (Shavelson 1976, Shavelson and Stern 1981). The teacher assumes responsibility for the content, strategies, and decisions that orchestrate the complex implementation of effective teaching. Further, the teacher takes responsibility for professional work with colleagues, the school community, and the profession. In an evaluation system in which teachers are seen as professionals, the focus is on the degree to which teachers are competent at professional problem finding and solving. The school administrator is seen as a leader among leaders in the collaborative work of schooling. If the work of teaching is thinking, then the evaluation of teaching is the evaluation of thinking.

To What Degree Can an Evaluation System Match Conditions Necessary for the Successful Operation of a Teacher Evaluation System?

A fourth decision for a district is whether it is ready to meet the conditions that are essential for an effective evaluation system. We concur with Darling-Hammond et al., the editors of the RAND report, and their identification of essential criteria.

1. All actors in the system must have a shared understanding of the criteria and processes for teacher evaluation.

2. All actors understand how these criteria and processes relate to the dominant symbols of the organization. There is a shared sense that they capture the most important aspects of teaching, that the evaluation system is consonant with educational goals and conceptions of teaching work.

3. Teachers perceive that the evaluation procedure enables and motivates them to improve their performance; principals perceive that the procedure enables them to provide instructional leadership.

4. All actors in the system perceive that the evaluation procedure allows them to strike a balance between adaptation and adaptability, between stability

and flexibility, and that the procedure achieves a balance between control and autonomy.

To these four considerations, we would add a fifth.

5. There is clear delineation between and congruence among the teacher evaluation system and the other major components of a comprehensive professional development program—supervision, peer coaching, and staff development.

The Cognitive Development View of Evaluation

The cognitive development view of evaluation can be defined as the diagnosis and assessment of the teacher's capacity for self-modification. Capacity for self-modification is seen as a function of teachers' awareness of, engagement in, performance of, and improvement of their own cognitive processes of teaching. These cognitive processes occur before, during, and after teaching, as well as in the context of collegial and professional practice. We choose the word "capacity" to represent "ability to," including those abilities that as yet may be untapped. Capacity is being added to, and distinguished from, the prevailing notions of evaluation.

● Teacher competency: any single knowledge, skill, or professional value believed to be relevant to the successful practice of teaching.

● Teacher competence: a repertoire of competencies.

● Teacher performance: the application of competencies.

● Teacher effectiveness: the effect that the teacher's performance has on students.

While competency, performance, and effectiveness are nested goals of teacher development and a dimension of teacher capacity, the ability to perform the cognitive processes of teaching provides a clearer window to the invisible skills of teaching.

To more fully understand the concept of cognitive development evaluation, it is important to describe the cognitive processes of teaching, as well as the underlying assumptions that give meaning to the notion of capacity and capacity building.

1. All individuals have the capacity for self-modification. Whether or not this capacity is exercised is a function of the individual's commitment to self-improvement and the resources (time, talent, and money) of the school and district to bring about change. A district must decide if it is able and willing to bring the resources to bear to bring about teacher improvement.

2. Teachers are professionals. This means they do the professional work of finding and solving problems and exercising judgment. As professionals they desire and deserve evaluation procedures that involve them, are growth producing, and are intellectually stimulating and dignifying.

3. Work environments can either support capacity building or stagnation. Teacher isolation reduces the probability of cognitive development. Collegial interchange, discussions about teaching, collaborative solving of problems, and developing curriculum extend and accelerate teacher growth.

4. Teaching is thinking. Effective teaching involves the cognitive, perception, and decision-making strategies that teachers use as they plan, teach, analyze, evaluate (reflect), and apply improvements to their own teaching.

5. Administrators and others who evaluate teaching must possess a set of intellectual capacities and skills that enable them to assess, supervise, and evaluate the cognitive processes of teaching.

Equipped with these assumptions about teachers, teaching, the work environment, and evaluators, the next task is examining the cognitive processes of teaching. What are those cognitive, perceptual, and decision-making strategies to which we refer? Are they actually recognizable, describable, and, therefore, no longer invisible? We believe they are.

The Cognitive Processes of Instruction

From the work of cognitive psychologists and other researchers (Costa and Garmston 1985), there is emerging a view of ideal teachers in terms of their intellectual functioning and their effects on student performance (Jones et al. 1987, Joyce and Showers 1988, Glatthorn and Baron 1984, Feuerstein 1980, Sternberg 1984, Hunter 1979, Berliner 1984, Shulman 1987, Shavelson 1976, 1977, Shavelson and Stern, 1981). These characteristics of adult development are described as benchmarks in Figure 6.2. These ideals include such concepts as strategic teaching, autonomous cognition, self-modification, high abstraction, and commitment. Effective teachers are also characterized as operating at high stages of cognitive development (Piaget), moral development (Kohlberg), social development (Erickson), and ego development (Loevinger) (Sprinthall and Theis-Sprinthall 1983).

What is this process called thinking? How do we view the process of information processing that is a basis for teacher (and evaluator) decision making? Figure 6.3 summarizes many of the psychological and psychobiological concepts of human information processing. According to this model, the individual constantly interprets information in terms of what is already known. If a teacher can easily understand new information based on existing knowledge (assimilation), then there is no dissonance or challenge. If, however, the teacher cannot assimilate the new information, that information must be processed, more information collected, and the ultimate resolution tested for its fit with the teacher's reality (accommodation). Accommodation may be achieved by a modification of that reality either in one's self-view or world

Figure 6.2
Benchmarks: A Construct for Teacher Development

		ENTRY	TENURE	MASTER
L	**KNOWING**	acquiring knowledge that belongs to someone else episodic unrelated bits of information	translating emerging use of cognitive map relational memory increasing reper- toire of content	constructing intuitive declarative memory mastery of content conceptually stored
E				
A	**DOING**	isolated mechanical recipe implementation impulsive imitative	conscious action and choice moves are linked together acts out of repertoire	integration of actions internalized refinement and diffusion inventing
R				
N	**VALUING**	egocentric adoption of others' values/ethics dependence externalizes causal factors well defended	focus on learners exploration situational independence responsible openness to change	allocentric altruistic integrated interdependence sees self as causal agent commitment to self-modification
I				
N				
G	**THINKING**	externally stim- ulated absence of internal vision other-directed evaluation dependent	self and other initiated representational, symbolic imaging collaborative evaluation independent	autonomous mental rehearsal flexible, open self-evaluation abstract from experience interdependent

view. This process, not surprisingly, is called "learning" and entails knowing, doing, valuing, and thinking.

Teaching decisions fall into four categories that roughly parallel the model of intellectual functioning described above.

1. Planning, the pre-active stage, consists of all those cognitive processes performed in mental rehearsal before instruction. Planning involves making a relationship among multiple time frames: long-range, term, monthly, weekly, daily, and individual lesson (Clark and Yinger 1979). The processes take place in a number of settings, such as during exercise, driving, sleeping, and, of course, the pre-conference. A lesson plan is an artifact of planning. The "real" planning is revealed through the expression of certain recognizable indicators. Specifically, the teacher:

• States a relationship between this lesson and a long-range goal.

Figure 6.3
Information Processing

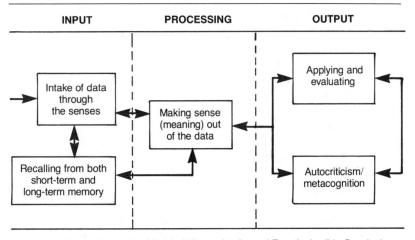

Source: A. Costa, "Towards a Model of Human Intellectual Functioning," in *Developing Minds: A Resource Book on Teaching Thinking* (Alexandria, Va.: Association for Supervision and Curriculum Development, 1984).

- Predicts student learnings that will result from the instruction.
- Envisions, describes, and sequences an instructional strategy (mental rehearsal) that includes content, time sequences, grouping/structuring, sequences of learning activities, repertoire of teacher behaviors, materials of instruction, and others as appropriate.
- Identifies data about entry level of students' previous learnings or capabilities.
- Displays conceptual knowledge of content.
- Anticipates a method of assessing student outcomes.

2. Teaching, the interactive stage, is the implementation of the plan, including all those decisions made while teaching (Saphier and Gowen 1982). A less rationally driven process than planning, teaching relies more on intuitive knowledge and "automatic" patterns of response behaviors. The proof of improved cognitive processing is in the classroom. Specifically, the teacher:

- Deals with multiple activities, styles, objectives, and outcomes simultaneously.
- Uses clear and precise language.
- Restrains impulsivity under stress.
- Monitors own progress along the instructional strategy.

- Is conscious of behavioral cues coming from students.
- Alters teaching strategy based upon cues coming from students.
- Routinizes classroom management tasks.
- Empathizes with feelings of students.

It is during teaching, of course, that data are collected that objectively describe the observable behaviors from which such thinking indicators are inferred. These behaviors usually include the ability to implement more than one objective and activity simultaneously, the alignment of instructional strategy to cognitive and affective outcomes (choosing an appropriate strategy from the four families of instruction), providing clear directions, working calmly and consistently with children, monitoring and adjusting their own behavior in response to clues from children, implementing classroom management tasks, and engaging with children in summary activities to discuss their own thinking and choice of strategies.

3. Analyzing and evaluating, the reflective stage, consists of the mental processes used to reflect upon, analyze, and judge teaching acts performed in the immediate past lesson. Analyzing involves collecting and using understandings derived from the comparison between actual and intended outcomes of teaching. If there is a great similarity between the desired behaviors predicted during the planning stage and those behaviors observed during the interactive stage, then there is a match and no discrepancy exists. If, however, there is a mismatch between the intended outcomes and the observed, then a discrepancy exists that must be resolved or explained. This is the meat of the learning about instruction, the basis for analysis and drawing cause-effect relationships (Barr and Brown 1971, Rohrkemper 1982). Specifically, teachers:

- Recall data about student behavior during the lesson.
- Recall data about their behaviors during the lesson.
- Compare intended and actual outcomes.
- Compare intended and actual instructional behaviors.
- Make causal relationships as to why objectives were or were not achieved.
- Display internal locus of control (self-responsibility).
- Self-evaluate their actions, planning, accuracy of lesson goals, teaching strategies, and specific behaviors.

4. Applying, the projective stage, involves learning from the teaching experience. As a result of the analysis and evaluation phase, teachers plan for and make commitments to their future actions. This stage involves abstracting generalizations from the analysis of their teaching experiences and carrying those generalizations to future situations. The teacher predicts the consequences of possible alternatives and is capable of playing those out in mental rehearsal. This step closes the instructional cycle because it is a basis for future planning. In applying, the teacher:

- Predicts or hypothesizes differences in learning outcomes if alternative strategies were to be used.
- Plans future lesson strategies based upon principles abstracted from the analysis of this lesson.
- Makes commitments to alter/experiment with new behaviors and strategies.
- Identifies inner resources needed for future successes.
- Seeks further assistance in learning and obtaining feedback.

These are many, but certainly not all, of the cognitive processes involved in these four components of teaching. The research on teacher cognition supports the assertion that the evaluation of teaching should include the assessment of the thought processes of teaching. We are further persuaded that a focus on enhancing teacher's thinking capacities will, in turn, increase student learning.

These thinking capacities are evidenced in the classroom, in interaction with colleagues outside of the classroom, and in the wider professional community.

Evaluation in Differing Arenas

If teacher evaluation is to serve as a set of tools to ascertain competencies and capabilities and create conditions for continuing growth, it is important to understand that the work of teachers occurs within several arenas, or contexts. These arenas define and influence how knowledge is obtained, processed, and used, as well as how the teacher grows in cognitive complexity. Teachers need support and challenge in the classroom, collegial interaction, and the profession as a whole to develop fully. The classroom, colleague, and profession are three arenas for the maturation of teachers (Kaufman and Hopkins 1987, Lambert 1987).

The Classroom Arena

During the first stages of a teacher's career, learning takes place primarily in the context of the classroom. The teacher's knowledge base is technical, mechanical, and often fragmented. A teacher's orientation to the world is often more focused on self, prompting such questions as "Can I do it?"; "What do I do?"; or "How can I survive?" The intellectual functions exhibited include decisions about lesson objectives, outcome, strategies, assessment, and trying to remember those plans. The sources of these behaviors are models from teacher training institutions, master teachers, memorable teachers as far back as grade school, and the teacher's subconscious learning styles.

155

During this time, dependency needs are often not mediated by collegial support because there are limited opportunities for interaction, feedback, and mirroring behaviors by a trusted colleague. If this confinement continues over time, teachers burn out or leave the profession. A paradox exists: Schools do not benefit from the richness and leadership that teachers can offer because they are organized to ensure this form of isolation. However, the full flavor and quality of an autonomous teacher is within teachers' grasp if they attend to the opportunities in the next two arenas.

The Arena of Collegial Practice

If the maturation process is to bloom, teachers need to learn with and from each other. It is within the arena of collegial practice that the intellectual functions of teaching are learned and deepened, since it is with colleagues that reflection is made possible. Vygotsky (1978) points out that the higher functions actually originate within this arena:

Every function in . . . cultural development appears twice: first, on the social level, and later on the individual level; first between people (interpsychological), and then inside (intrapsychological). This applies equally to voluntary attention, to logical memory, and to the formation of concepts. All the higher functions originate as actual relationships between individuals.

Together, individuals create and discuss ideas, eliciting thinking that surpasses individual effort. As individuals engage in problem-solving, conversation, and coaching, multiple perspectives are expressed, dissonance created and reduced, discrepancies perceived and resolved, alternatives weighted, options selected, and consequences considered and evaluated. As teachers gain experience together, they select, integrate, and develop intricate, automatic patterns of behavior much like the driver who can effortlessly execute a quick turn to avoid a collision. The parameters of thought are broadened by these processes, and concepts are also shepherded and stabilized. Reality is tested, while changing perspectives of reality take on new meanings about teaching. Teachers no longer talk only about "my kids, my room, my chalk" but about "our kids, our school, our community." Thus, teacher efficacy is achieved (Berman and McClaughlin 1977).

At first, this may seem like an orderly process. Lieberman (1985), however, reminds us that collaboration is a messy undertaking, requiring tolerance for ambiguity, commitment, flexibility, and room for error. Any evaluation system that promotes teacher development cannot confine itself to classroom performance; it must attend to indicators that collegial interaction is being sought, nurtured, and used.

Clearly, collegiality is the common ground upon which the culture of a school and district is built. We are not going to get smarter or better at what we do without a healthy and continued dose of collegial practice. Indeed, adult development is not automatic, but a function of collegiality and the self-reflection that is made possible through the reflection pool in a colleague's eyes (Lambert 1983).

Thoughtful Contributions to the Profession

Once the teacher sees the relationship of the self to the broader community, the context for learning and contributing expands even further. This is the arena of the profession as a whole. This broadened perspective engenders attention to the school, community, society, and profession. The shifting horizon means interest in the consequences of actions in this larger arena, as well as commitment and responsibility for these consequences. In addition to "our kids, our school, our community," questions of major magnitude arise.

1. What is the purpose of schooling?
2. What will the next generation of teachers be like?
3. What is the role of schooling from a global perspective?
4. How will schools address issues of social conditions, interdependence, and cultural diversity?
5. How can I contribute to the profession and to society?
6. What legacy will I leave?
7. How might the role of teacher be redefined through reform, legislation, and policy?
8. How will schools be led?
9. What leadership can I best provide?

To address these questions, teachers construct and distribute knowledge through action research, persuasion, and publication. In their teaching roles, teachers develop increasingly wide and specialized patterns of repertoire that are stored in long-term memory. These patterns of strategies become automatic, freeing the mind to perform increasingly complex and influential roles as mentor, teacher-in-residence, teacher advisor, lead teacher, career teacher, master teacher, and member of a leadership team.

We have seen this play enacted: Teachers begin working together, taking initiative, and providing leadership as they seek to influence and improve the quality of schooling. They revisit their compelling urge to make a difference. The payoffs to their districts are profound. Teachers take responsibility for developing a workable evaluation system. They figure out how to schedule coaching into their lives. Teacher association members begin to talk about policy trust agreements and non-confrontational bargaining and giving attention to professional development. Mature teachers voluntarily take responsibility for the mentoring and enculturation of new teachers. Leadership teams confront and solve troublesome problems and invite parents to engage with them in the complex and challenging struggle of educating today's youth. The culture of schooling takes on a sense of community, that we're all in this together.

We find that there are districts that enjoy relationships and conditions that are growth producing for professionals, children, and parents. A few of the indicators that such a professional environment is in place are shown in Figure 6.4.

Within each of these arenas—the classroom, collegial practice, and the profession—there are activities in which effective teachers engage. And there are artifacts from which an evaluator may draw inferences about the teacher's developing cognitive functions. There are also benchmarks by which an individual, an evaluator, an evaluation team, and a district can assess whether individuals are developing toward higher levels of human development.

Figure 6.4
Examples of Cognitive Development Artifacts

Instructional Stages

- Explicit intellectual behaviors during pre-conference, teaching and post-conference
- Lesson plans
- Letters to parents, students, community
- Criterion-referenced tests
- New teacher journals
- Teacher-made instructional materials
- Other

Collegial Practice

- Common language
- Action plans, instructional plans, curricular plans, assessment plans
- Demonstration teaching, coteaching, team teaching
- Textbook requests, staff development requests
- Study outline
- Action research findings, syntheses of research
- Coaching schedules
- Statement of learnings by teachers
- Agendas
- Peer data as part of evaluation portfolio
- Other

Professional Contributions

- Membership on leadership teams, governance groups
- Alternative role descriptions
- Plans for working with new teachers or for facilitating coaching programs
- Agenda of workshops planned, presented
- Establishment of professional library, data bases for telecommunication
- Publication of articles, research findings
- Data about performance collected from students parents, peers, community
- Policy statements, community plans
- Volunteer plans
- Other

Benchmarks: How Do We Know if Teachers Are Thinking More Intelligently?

Earlier we referred to a construct for understanding the learning process. We described "learning" as a function of knowing, doing, valuing, and thinking. Figure 6.2 (p. 152) is a construct for further understanding the maturation process in each of these realms. This construct presumes several relationships and dynamics: first, that knowing, doing, valuing, and thinking are inextricably intertwined and together constitute learning. The "capacity for self-modification," as we have used it, is a process that is crippled unless all dimensions are growing.

Traditional evaluation systems, at their very best, have focused on "knowing" and "doing." "Valuing" has been the shadow area that influences and frustrates but is rarely made explicit. Yet valuing is the driving force that gives perspective and intention to thinking and action. "Thinking" has been the missing link. Development in thinking contributes to development in all the other areas, including valuing.

Second, teachers may differ from one another dramatically in entry-level characteristics related to valuing and thinking. They will develop at unique rates and in relation to the dynamics of their school environment (Ryan 1979).

Third, we believe we can relate this construct to an evaluation instrument (Figure 6.5) that enables districts to consider how maturation relates to improving teacher performance and informing personnel decisions such as granting tenure. For instance, if a teacher ready for tenure is not exhibiting many of the characteristics in the tenure column in Figure 6.2, this should signal a need for the formal consideration of dismissal and collection of additional data to corroborate or refute these assumptions. Individuals who exhibit characteristics in the third column are those who should be considered for advancement into teacher leadership roles and master teacher status. Please note that we suggest these as signals, rather than as certainties. We cannot anticipate the process of human development with a degree of certainty that would justify legal or quasi-legal decisions.

We suggest one other use for the construct in Figure 6.2. Teachers and administrators may find it useful as a means to:

1. Decide who will be involved in the design and implementation process. We recommend broad and public participation. The majority of the group should be teachers (chosen by teachers), including representatives of the professional association. The group should also comprise principals, district-office personnel who have the authority to negotiate the process through the board and the collective bargaining process, and community or parent representatives. In the final measure, this group will lend legitimacy to the process.

2. Educate staff members in the intent of evaluation, past practices, and the relation of cognitive development evaluation to teaching performance. Because the design group needs to sponsor and participate in the education of the whole staff in the nature of cognitive development evaluation, they must be thoroughly knowledgeable and convinced about the value of this direction. To make sense to people, cognitive development evaluation needs to be compatible with other goals in the district: student thinking, peer coaching, or supervision. If the goal of developing student thinking is emphasized in the

Figure 6.5
Cognitive Development Evaluation Form

TEACHER'S NAME _____ EVALUATOR _____ DATE _____

SCHOOL _____ GRADE/SUBJECT _____

COGNITIVE ATTRIBUTE: I. PLANNING (PREACTIVE STAGE) OBSERVABLE INDICATORS	OFTEN	SOMETIMES	NOT YET
1. States relationship between this lesson and a long-range goal.			
2. Predicts student learnings that will result from this instruction.			
3. Envisions, describes, and sequences an instructional strategy which includes: (Mental Rehearsal) _____ Content _____ Time sequences _____ Grouping/structuring _____ Sequences of learning activities _____ Repertoire of teacher behaviors _____ Materials of instruction _____ Other			
4. Identifies data about entry level of students/previous learnings/ capabilities.			
5. Displays conceptual knowledge of content.			
6. Anticipates a method of assessing outcomes.			

COGNITIVE ATTRIBUTE: II. TEACHING (INTERACTIVE STAGE)	OFTEN	SOMETIMES	NOT YET
OBSERVABLE INDICATORS			
7. Deals with multiple activities, styles, objectives, outcomes simultaneously.			
8. Uses clear and precise language.			
9. Restrains impulsivity under stress.			
10. Monitors own progress along the instructional strategy (metacognition).			
11. Is conscious of behavioral cues coming from students (read and flex).			
12. Alters teaching strategy based on cues coming from students.			
13. Routinizes the classroom management tasks.			
14. Demonstrates empathy (allocentrism).			

COGNITIVE ATTRIBUTE: III. ANALYZING AND EVALUATING (REFLECTIVE STAGE)	OFTEN	SOMETIMES	NOT YET
OBSERVABLE INDICATORS			
15. Recalls data about student behavior during the lesson.			
16. Recalls data about teaching behaviors during the lesson.			
17. Makes comparisons between intended and actual outcomes.			
18. Makes comparisons between intended and actual instructional behaviors.			
19. Makes causal relationships as to why objectives were/were not achieved.			
20. Displays internal locus of control.			
21. Self-evaluates own actions, planning, accuracy of lesson goals, teaching strategies, specific behaviors (autocriticism).			

Continued

Figure 6.5 (continued)

COGNITIVE ATTRIBUTE: IV. APPLYING (PROJECTIVE STAGE) OBSERVABLE INDICATORS	OFTEN	SOMETIMES	NOT YET
22. Predicts or hypothesizes differences in learning outcomes if alternate strategies were to be used.			
23. Plans future lessons strategies based upon principles abstracted from the analysis of this lesson.			
24. Makes commitment to alter/experiment with new behaviors and strategies.			
25. Identifies inner resources needed for future successes.			
26. Seeks further assistance in learning and obtaining feedback.			

curricular and instructional processes, cognitive development evaluation will be a natural outgrowth.

3. Define the purposes and criteria for the evaluation system. The design group will want to consider the four major purposes of teacher evaluation and the RAND Criteria, modifying and adding their own. We suggest that districts decide which purposes to pursue and then select evaluation criteria. Continual communication should occur with the entire staff to secure ideas and feedback.

4. Design the evaluation forms and procedures. The evaluation forms presented in Figures 6.5 and 6.6 suggest that evaluators be open to the range of opportunities to gather data about the performance of a range of cognitive behaviors in a variety of settings—in the classroom, in school meetings, in lesson planning, in pre- and post-conferencing, and even beyond the school environment. We suggest that there are three forms, one for each of the major professional roles the teacher plays: as a classroom teacher, as a member of a collegial team, and as a member of the profession.

Since the intent of cognitive development evaluation is to judge the degree to which teachers engage in, perform, and continue to improve in their instructionally related intellectual functions, the evaluation forms presented in Figures 6.5. and 6.6 are designed for that purpose. They list the cognitive processes of the four phases of teaching—planning, teaching, analyzing and

Figure 6.5 (continued)

COGNITIVE ATTRIBUTE:	V. COLLEGIAL MEMBER OF A SCHOOL TEAM	OFTEN	SOMETIMES	NOT YET
OBSERVABLE INDICATORS				
1. Engages in conversations about teaching.				
2. Participates in faculty and/or district groups for purposes of design, implementation and support of activities such as:				
• Focused study on selected topics				
• Follow-up groups to support instructional inservice				
• Problem-solving				
• Curriculum development				
• Action Research				
• Other _____				
3. Engages in peer support systems such as:				
• Demonstration teaching, coteaching, team teaching				
• Peer coaching				
• Mentoring				
• Peer review				
• Peer evaluation				
• Intensive support to "at-risk" colleagues				
• Other _____				

evaluating, and applying—as well as cognitive indicators performed as a member of a collegial team and as a member of the profession.

Typical evaluation forms require evaluators to make a value judgment (e.g., outstanding, satisfactory, or unsatisfactory) or a rating (1-5) about the teacher's overt performance. Because the system we've described is intended to assess the development of these intellectual skills, the columns "Often," "Sometimes," and "Not Yet" imply a direction of growth. It expresses faith that the teacher is growing and has the capacity to continually employ and refine these intelligent behaviors.

If a given decision point, such as tenure or promotion, is arrived at and a majority of "not yet" checks are noted, a decision will need to be made about the district's intention for dismissal. At that time, specific procedures, timelines, and responsibilities unique to each district should be implemented.

Figure 6.6
Cognitive Evaluation Form

COGNITIVE ATTRIBUTE: CONTRIBUTIONS TO THE PROFESSION OBSERVABLE INDICATORS	OFTEN	SOMETIMES	NOT YET
1. Engages in leadership activities.			
2. Exercises career options.			
3. Designs and/or provides professional development.			
4. Establishes information systems.			
5. Conducts action research.			
6. Publishes observations, insights, findings.			
7. Evaluates own performance.			
8. Identifies problems in schooling, society.			
9. Influences, designs, evaluates public policy			
10. Volunteers to mediate problems, conditions.			
11. Other _____			

However, we would like to suggest a couple of guidelines in critical areas.

Keep in mind that the responsibility to provide intellectually stimulating professional development practices is with the district. It is not enough to hire and evaluate teachers to keep the good ones and cut out the poor ones. We have a professional obligation to help teachers to be as good as they can be, and we must invest the time and money in them before termination. Major strides in teacher growth and development are more likely to be realized through efforts in supervision, coaching, and staff development than in evaluation. We strongly recommend that the major resources of the district focus in these areas, complemented by cognitive development evaluation, not driven by it. Figure 6.7 provides an example of a narrative evaluation using the cognitive development evaluation concepts. The current practices that have been legislated in several states in which evaluation is the centerpiece have

Figure 6.7
A Narrative Evaluation of Teacher Cognition

Mark is a first-year, 7th grade math teacher at the middle school in our district. He is an introspective, self-prescribing, self-sufficient, self-analyzing, autonomous teacher. In planning lessons, Mark considers the place of the new skill in the overall plan for the unit. He selects teaching strategies appropriate for the lessons and is conscious of the sequence of activities. For example, in working with integers, he first taught the students the importance of knowing the number line. He had each class paint a number line on the floor on each side of the room. This knowledge of the number line would help them in learning to add and subtract integers. When teaching addition and subtraction, Mark asked students to refer to the number lines they had made.

Mark also bases his lessons on the previous learning of the students and considers ways to assess student success. During one of the lessons I observed Mark teach, he provided a 20-minute review session. He said he wanted to give students who had not mastered the addition and subtraction of integers extra time to practice with his guidance. The students who had learned the skill were provided with more challenging problems.

Mark also handles multiple activities with ease. During one lesson, he began class with a word problem that required students to use the skills he had taught them on problem solving. He asked students to think about this problem throughout the class period (during the other activities when they had a moment), and it would be the first question on the "candy" game at the end of the period. The problem remained on the overhead screen for the remainder of the period. Mark went on with his lesson. At certain times during the class, he asked if anyone had solved the problem. In addition to having this problem solving challenge, he had one student who had been absent using the construction paper and scissors to make a personal number line.

Mark monitors his students, adjusts instruction to student needs, has clear classroom procedures, and is emphatic with students. Throughout the class period, Mark monitors his students' behavior and their progress. He has the ability to work with individual students and to supervise the activities of the other students at the same time. Mark has routinized his class procedures and now uses an agenda to guide him and the students in this routine. Students understand classroom rules, procedures, and consequences. Throughout the solving of difficult problems, Mark demonstrates empathy with the cognitive struggles of the students. He does this by using a few well-placed words when students have come to a wrong answer. His response to them is one of understanding, stating how he has felt or done the same thing. He is accepting of student answers, whether right or wrong, and focuses his attention on the process of thinking. When a student gives an answer that is incorrect, he shows he respects the thinking process. For example, he might say, "Let's see if that is correct by acting out the solution." Students demonstrate a freedom to express their thinking without a fear or failure.

Mark is field sensitive. He is, for the most part, cognizant of the reactions and comprehension of the students and adjusts the instruction accordingly. He expresses confidence in the students' ability, provides continual guidance, gives clear lesson presentations, models the skills, and humanizes the math curriculum. He also talks about specific outcomes, discusses lessons in separate discrete steps, and considers observable evidence to verify that students have achieved the objective. Mark is able to analyze, evaluate, and modify his own behaviors and teaching strategies in response to student reactions. Mark gives his best to teaching; he is a professional.

crowded out supervision, coaching, and staff development and created an unbalanced, fear-infused, and largely ineffective system.

As we have noted, an evaluation system that challenges, intellectually stimulates, and honors teachers as professionals must engage them in the process of judging their own performance. We recommend a process that considers alternative ways of deciding who makes the judgments about performance. Most systems do not even consider this question, assuming that those in authority automatically judge. We suggest that external judgment is far less growth producing than internal judgment in cases where teachers are capable of self-judgment; in fact, it may well get in the way of growth. Glickman's directionality continuum for developmental supervision (1980) can be used to consider issues of judgment (Figure 6.8).

Some districts are considering alternative judgment processes based on district-defined "autonomy," using developmental criteria or professional contributions as the basis, or allowing each individual with a satisfactory evaluation under the previous system to begin collaborative or self-directed evaluation. New teachers are given added support from a mentor or master teacher and judged by an administrator or administrator-peer team until the tenure decision is reached. In some systems, administrative evaluation has been replaced for most teachers by self-evaluation in concert with extensive peer coaching practices (Garmston and Eblen 1988, Ludwig and Raddeau 1987).

We strongly recommend that whatever forms or procedures your district adopts have your entire staff's brand so they feel ownership and commitment to the process.

5. Identify the artifacts to be used as evidence of cognitive development. Since only some of the intellectual functions will occur in the presence of an evaluator, or will need corroboration, we recommend that the design group develop a list of appropriate "artifacts" (Figure 6.4, p. 158). By artifact we mean external evidence that signals or manifests growth into the desired cognitive functions. A few examples are in Figure 6.4. Please note that the

Figure 6.8
Continuum of Evaluation Judgments

TEACHER		
		SUPERVISOR
high teacher judgment high teacher autonomy	collaborative judgment	high supervisor judgment low teacher autonomy

lists are not mutually exclusive; artifacts in one area may serve in several areas. Teachers can select among these artifacts and others to fit their professional goals as well as the goals of the school and district. And these artifacts can be collected by teachers and administrators as they go about their work.

6. Design long-range program monitoring and assessment processes. The design group may wish to continue their work to monitor and assess the progress of the program, or they may appoint a subcommittee to do so. You can expect that the system will self-adjust, taking on the characteristics of your district. Be alert to a few developments:

• Alterations that are in line with your original purposes and criteria signaling a positive response and evidence of institutionalization.

• Alterations that shift toward the former practice or non-practice of your previous system. In the latter case, the monitoring group can intervene to steer the system back in line with your original intent.

• An escalation of energy spent gathering cognitive evaluation artifacts or lines of evidence. In some systems, increasing energy will go to data gathering instead of data use. This may be a signal about too much teacher stress about the system and is a cue for a reassessment of practices and alignment with original intentions.

Information about the progress of the system can be obtained by interviewing; observing; reading evaluation forms, narratives, and portfolios; and monitoring timelines, student achievement data, and school culture indicators.

Additionally, teacher satisfaction with any evaluation system is strongly related to:

• Perceptions that all evaluators share the same criteria for evaluation.

• Frequent sampling of teacher performance.

• Frequent communication and feedback.

• Their ability to affect the criteria for evaluation (Natriello and Dornbusch 1980-81).

These four guidelines, therefore, can also be employed by the monitoring group to ensure continued satisfaction and effectiveness.

7. Preparation of evaluators and teachers in the process. It will not surprise you that evaluators also must possess well-developed thought processes to function effectively in that role as well as other leadership roles. The cognitive levels of the evaluators or supervisors are closely related to their leadership style. Principals who have achieved higher levels of complex conceptual development have been perceived by their teachers as more flexible in problem-solving, more responsive, less rigid, and less authoritarian.

The cognitive development process of evaluation demands that the evaluator exercise certain mental functions: having an ideal image or standard clearly in mind, gathering data from many sources and arenas, comparing data with the standard, making inferences and judgments, communicating data with precision and accuracy, using data for further decision making, and striving to learn more about and to refine one's own skills in the evaluation process. Furthermore, the process implies that evaluators hold simultaneously goals for the teacher, other staff members, the school, the district, and schooling in general. These are extraordinary expectations and require preparation. The teachers who are to be evaluated must be prepared as well. Individuals must have opportunities to learn what is intended by any evaluation system. This implies training, time for dialogue about the meaning of cognitive development for teaching, and self-reflection about one's relationship to intellectual functions. Teacher preparation programs must also provide supervision that systematically supports and accelerates the development of teacher cognition.

Cognitive coaching (Costa and Garmston 1985) is a professional development approach that enables participants to recognize, perform, and coach for the cognitive processes of teaching. Other training approaches can be designed by individuals knowledgeable in cognition by using the observable indicators as a training outline.

8. Align school and district policies and practices with the philosophy and intention of cognitive development evaluation. A healthy, professional organizational culture is one in which the mission and goals of the district are aligned with the policies and daily practices. This alignment is paramount to trust and essential to the effective implementation of any program. We further suggest that the philosophy contained in the mission statement needs to respect children and adults and express confidence in their capacities for self-direction and self-modification. As your district works to accomplish its mission and to support the development of children and adults, it is useful to examine what factors are a catalyst for empowerment and to identify those activities, experiences, and relationships that enable individuals to come into fuller possession of personal power. Since the empowered individual has the capacity for self-modification, we are persuaded that the major goal of an evaluation system is not just to judge what is, but to nurture and support what could be. Support takes the form of providing teachers options, choice, authority, and responsibility. And evaluation must be contextualized into a "user friendly" organizational culture that allows for these four factors. Otherwise, the culture will reject the evaluation system as a biological system would reject a foreign virus.

It might be useful to provide a few core policy statements that exemplify such an organizational design. Compare these with our recommended steps for developing an evaluation system, and you will discover the beliefs-policy-practice alignment to which we refer.

• The District Evaluation Task Force shall consist of a district office representative, principals, a majority of teachers, and a parent or community representative. The Task Force will design and implement the teacher evaluation system.

• Administrators and teachers will share responsibility for the collection of multiple forms of evaluation data in three major areas: classroom, collegial practice, and professional practice.

• Professional development opportunities will be made available to administrators and teachers. Such opportunities will enable our district educators to pursue learning in areas related to personal goals, school goals, and district goals.

• Time and other discretionary resources will be made available to teachers and administrators so that they may pursue their goals. Resources will be allocated by the Professional Development Committee at each school based on criteria created by each staff.

• Minimums and full days will be made available for use in professional development activities. This will include up to _____minimum days and up to _____full days.

• Teachers will have opportunities for advancement into roles with increasing leadership responsibilities and duties. Such roles will include intern, career teacher, master teacher, mentor teacher, and other roles designed by the district in cooperation with the staff.

These policy statements can be the genesis for options, choice, authority, and responsibility in your district. Emancipation is "an achievement, not an endowment" (Greene 1987), and educators must choose to take advantage of opportunities for use in their own development. And, we are persuaded that the majority of educators still have that spark of excitement for the profession that drew them to teaching in the first place and that growth toward continued self-modification will take place within an opportunity-rich environment.

Summary

One of the great myths in our profession has been that teacher evaluation practices have improved instruction for students. Most district evaluation policies have that statement within their preambles. We have virtually no evidence that this is the case (Glickman 1986).

Cognitive development evaluation offers you an opportunity to retain that statement in your preamble and possibly to realize that goal for your district. There is significant evidence that teachers who function at the higher levels of human development assist students to achieve academically, cooperate, possess higher self-confidence, solve problems, think creatively and critically, and function as self-directing individuals. These are the skills that our students need now and for the 21st century.

Cognitive development evaluation is designed to help teachers increase and perform the intellectual functions of teaching, thereby developing their capacities for self-modification. Such teachers are in the process of self-learning through increased maturation in knowing, doing, valuing, and thinking. These teachers are getting better all the time.

We have invited you to examine with us the district's opportunity and responsibility to create environments in which everyone is in the process of learning. This engagement is a moral imperative, calling into question the very purposes upon which schooling is based. We hope that we have assisted you to reframe your thinking about evaluation; and perhaps we have even assisted you to reframe your thinking about schooling. Modest goals? Of course not. Altering how teachers and administrators think about their craft is a bold undertaking.

References

Barr, R., and V.L. Brown. "Evaluation and Decision Making." *The Reading Teacher* 24, 4 (1971).

Berliner, D.C. "The Half Full Glass: A Review of the Research in Teaching." In *What We Know about Teaching*, edited by P. Hosford. Alexandria, Va.: Association for Supervision and Curriculum Development, 1984.

Berman, P., and M.W. McLaughlin. "Factors Affecting Implementation and Continuation." *Federal Programs Supporting Educational Change*. Vol. 7. Santa Monica, Calif.: The Rand Corporation, 1977.

Calhoon, E.F. "Relationship of Teachers' Perceptions of Prescriptive and Descriptive Observations of Teaching by Instructional Supervisors." *Georgia Educational Leadership*. 1985.

Clark, C., and R. Yinger. "Teachers' Thinking." In *Research on Teaching*, edited by P. Peterson and H. Walberg. Berkeley, Calif.: McCutchan Publishers, 1979.

Costa, A. "Towards a Model of Human Intellectual Functioning." In *Developing Minds: A Resource Book on Teaching Thinking*, edited by A. Costa. Alexandria, Va.: Association for Supervision and Curriculum Development, 1984.

Costa, A., and R. Garmston. "Supervision for Intelligent Teaching." *Educational Leadership* 42 (February 1985): 70-80.

Darling-Hammond, L., A.E. Wise, and S.R. Pease. "Teacher Evaluation in the Organizational Context: A Review of the Literature." *Review of Educational Research* 53 (Fall 1983).

Feuerstein, R. *Instrumental Enrichment*. Baltimore: University Park Press, 1980.

Garmston, R., and D. Eblen. "Visions, Decisions and Results: Changing School Culture through Staff Development." *Journal of Staff Development* (Spring 1988).

Glatthorn, A., and J. Baron. "The Good Thinker." In *Developing Minds: A Resource Book for Teaching Thinking*, edited by A. Costa. Alexandria, Va.: Association for Supervision and Curriculum Development, 1984.

Glickman, C. *Developmental Supervision: Alternative Approaches to Helping Teachers Improve Instruction*. Alexandria, Va.: Association for Supervision and Curriculum Development, 1980.

Glickman, C. *Supervision of Instruction: A Developmental Approach.* Newton, Mass.: Allyn & Bacon, 1985.

Glickman, C. "Supervision for Increasing Teacher Thought and Commitment." National Curriculum Study Institute presentation, New Orleans, March, 1986.

Greene, M. Personal Conversation with Linda Lambert. New York, December 30, 1987.

Harvey, O.J. "Conceptual Systems and Attitude Change." In *Attitude, Ego Involvement and Change,* edited by C. Sherif and M. Sherif. New York: Wiley, 1967.

Hunt, D.E., and B.R. Joyce. "Teacher Trainer Personality and Initial Teaching Style." *American Educational Research Journal* (1967).

Hunter, M. "Teaching is Decision Making." *Educational Leadership* 37 (October 1979): 62-68.

Jones, B.F., A.S. Palinscar, D.S. Ogle, and E.G. Carr. *Strategic Teaching and Learning: Cognitive Instruction in the Content Areas.* Alexandria, Va.: Association for Supervision and Curriculum Development, 1987.

Joyce, B., and B. Showers. *Student Achievement Through Staff Development.* New York: Longman Press, 1988.

Kaufman, B., and P. Hopkins. "An Ecology of Professional Development." The Professional Development Project. Marin County, California, 1987.

Lambert, L. "A Critical Analysis of Assumptions Held by Staff Developers, Researchers and Policy Makers about Adult Learning." Doctoral diss., University of San Francisco, 1983.

Lambert, L. "Self-Reflection and Collegiality: Critical Aspects of Adult Development." Speech. Phi Delta Kappan Leadership Institute, Denver, November, 1987.

Lieberman, A. "Enhancing School Improvement through Collaboration." Paper prepared for the Allerton Symposium on Illinois Educational Improvement, June, 1985.

Ludwig, B., and J. Raddeau. "In Our Own Voices: The Ross Valley Evaluation System." Marin County, California, Office of Education, October, 1987.

Natriello, G., and S.M. Dornbusch. "Pitfalls in the Evaluation of Teachers by Principals." *Administrators Notebook* 29, 6 (1980-81).

Rohrkemper, M. "Teacher Self-Assessment." In *Helping Teachers Manage Classrooms,* edited by D. Duke. Alexandria, Va.: Association for Supervision and Curriculum Development, 1982.

Ryan, K. "Stages for Teacher Growth." Presentation. Association for Supervision and Curriculum Development, 1979.

Saphier, J., and R. Gower. *The Skillful Teacher: Building Your Teaching Skills.* Carlisle, Mass.: Research for Better Teaching, Inc., 1982.

Sergiovanni, T., and J. Corbally, eds. *Leadership and Organizational Culture.* Urbana and Chicago: University of Illinois Press, 1986.

Shavelson, R. "Teacher Decision Making." In *Psychology of Teaching Methods: 1976 Yearbook of the National Society for the Study of Education,* Part I. Chicago: University of Chicago Press, 1976.

Shavelson, R. "Teacher Sensitivity to the Reliability of Information in Making Pedagogical Decisions." *American Educational Research Journal* 14 (Spring 1977).

Shavelson, R., and P. Stern. "Research on Teachers' Pedagogical Thoughts, Judgments, Decisions and Behaviors." *Review of Educational Research* 51 (1981).

Shulman, L. "Knowledge and Teaching: Foundations of the New Reforms." *Harvard Educational Review* 57 (February 1987).

Sprinthall, N., and L. Theis-Sprinthall. "The Teacher as an Adult Learner: A Cognitive Development View." In *Staff Development: Eighty-Second Yearbook of the National Society for the Study of Education*, Part II, edited by Gary Griffin. Chicago: University of Chicago Press, 1983.

Sternberg, R. *Beyond IQ: A TRIARCHIC Theory of Human Intelligence.* New York: Cambridge University Press, 1984.

Vygotsky, L.S. *Society of Mind.* Cambridge, Mass.: Harvard University Press, 1978.

Witherall, C.S., and V.L. Erickson. "Teacher Education as Adult Development." *Theory into Practice* (June 1978).